P9-AGO-001

how to catch bottomfish

Charles White

With A Special Section By
SIDNEY S. GIRLING

Illustrated by Nelson Dewey

Cover photos by Bob Jones

HERITAGE HOUSE PUBLISHING COMPANY LTD.
Box 1228, Station A
Surrey, B.C. V3S 2B3

Canadian Cataloguing in Publication Data
White, Charles 1925-
  How to Catch Bottomfish

  Originally published: Sidney, B.C.:
Saltaire, 1971.
  ISBN 0-88896-192-8

  1. Bottom Fishing.   I. Title   II. Series.
SH455.6.W55   799.1'6   C86-091077-6

Printed in Canada

ABOUT THE AUTHOR

Charlie White is an internationally known author, film maker, television personality, and fish behavior researcher.

He has written nine books on salmon and marine life, with sales over 400,000 copies, making him among the leading authors on salmon fishing. His latest book is Charlie White's 101 Fishing Secrets. His first book, How to Catch Salmon: Basic Fundamentals, has sold more than 130,000 copies. He is co-author of a new university textbook, Fisheries Harvesting Life from Water, being used for courses at the University of Washington and other colleges.

In 1973, he began experimenting with a remote-controlled under-water television camera to study salmon strike behavior. His under-water close-ups, in freeze frame and slow motion, revealed for the first time many fascinating new facts about how salmon and other species approach and strike various lures.

He has made three feature-length films about his work, two of which are now marketed on video cassette (Why Fish Strike and In Search of the Ultimate Lure). He has been recognized in Who's Who for his fish behavior studies. He has also invented a number of popular fishing products, including the Scotty Downrigger, Electric Hooksharp, and "The Lure" by Charlie White.

Articles on Charlie have appeared in major magazines and newspapers across North America. He has also had his own television series and is a frequent guest on radio and television talk shows. His syndicated feature, Charlie White's Fishing Tips, appears weekly in newspapers in Canada and U.S. In addition he conducts fishing seminars at col-

3

leges and in auditoriums throughout the Pacific Northwest and lectures several times a year at the University of Washington School of Fisheries.

Charlie lives on the water near Sidney, B.C., and continues his unique water research on fish strike behavior. Charlie lives on the waterfront near Sidney, B.C., and continues his unique underwater research on fish strike behavior. For more information write Charlie at 11046 Chalet Road, Sidney, B.C. V8L 4R4.

VERY IMPORTANT

In B.C. do not go fishing without first studying the current B.C. Tidal Waters Sport Fishing Guide, published annually by the Federal Department of Fisheries and Oceans. It is available free at sporting goods stores, marinas and similar outlets. The Guide contains all regulations governing sport fishing not only for salmon but also for halibut, rockfish, crabs, oysters and other species. Check carefully the sections on spot closures which were introduced as a conservation measure to protect not only salmon but also crabs, lingcod and many other species.

Also note that the multiple-hook rigs described on pages 57-60 are illegal in B.C. and some other Pacific Coast waters.

CONTENTS

INTRODUCTION

When we prepared our first booklet on bottom-fish we had no real idea of the number of persons interested enough to pay for information on the subject.

As this sixth printing goes to press in greatly expanded form (more than four times as much material as in the original edition) we are very gratified at the continuing response.

With the increasing pressure of our daily lives, a relaxing day on the water has strong appeal. We are very fortunate in the Northwest to have lots of open air and unpolluted water to enjoy.

In this book we deal with the best known of the edible saltwater fishes of the North Pacific coast.

(An exception is Salmon, covered in detail in Heritage House book, *How to Catch Salmon: Basic Fundamentals*. This popular book is a continuing best seller with sales now over 135,000.)

Most of these species dwell on or near the bottom (within five or six feet of the sand, mud, rock, or gravel). Perch are the exception. They are a midwater fish.

These fish are often scorned by sport fishermen who spend all of their time chasing (often futilely!) the more glamorous and spectacular fighting salmon. There is no doubt that catching a salmon is one of the peak experiences in the fishing world and makes the best material for "fish stories" back home or with the boys in the office. However, there are many, many times when the salmon just are not in your area or they stubbornly refuse to bite! (At

the best of times, the salmon will only feed a short time each day.)

At these times, the fisherman can either patiently fish for salmon with only a small chance of success — or try for bottomfish.

These bottom dwellers can provide lots of excitement and a very tasty meal to boot. Most species are delicious eating and many people prefer them to salmon.

To the great mass of freshwater fishermen in North America the bottomfish of the North Pacific ocean are bigger, harder fighting, and better eating than anything they have ever caught in fresh water!

" ...A TASTY MEAL TO BOOT."

Bottom fishing doesn't require expensive equipment. A simple single action reel, almost any kind of rod, some hooks and bait are all that are needed, especially for beginners.

You don't even need a boat for many types of bottomfish. Many can be taken right from the shore, especially on rocky drop-offs. Piers and wharves are also excellent locations for bottomfishing.

A small dinghy or aluminum boat with outboard will allow you to cover a lot of productive water. Some types of fish are found mostly in deep water and on sandy bottoms away from shorelines where it is impossible to reach from shore. You might build a raft and play Tom Sawyer to get to these fish, but rafts are difficult to handle, and can be very dangerous if the wind comes up.

Fishing from a boat has the added advantage of drifting effortlessly with wind or tide over a wide area while the shorebound angler can work only a very limited area of shore line where conditions are suitable.

The late Sidney Girling wrote a comprehensive section of this book outlining in meticulous detail the methods he used for catching bottomfish from a rowing dinghy. His detailed records of his many trips list impressive and consistent catches of bottomfish.

Mr. Girling specialized in fishing the rocky reefs and the majority of his catch has been rockfish and lingcod. However, he has also caught many other types of bottomfish. He even had an hour long battle with a huge halibut. A version of the octopus-type lure he developed and describes on page 116 is now available at sporting goods stores.

CHAPTER I

EQUIPMENT

You can catch bottomfish quite successfully using a handline, but an inexpensive rod and reel makes it easier and more fun. If a fish begins swimming toward the boat, it is awkward to keep proper tension with a handline.

A rod helps take the shock out of sudden lunges by the fish. It also gives you more control in guiding the line around and under the boat as the fish dashes frantically for freedom.

CHOOSING A ROD

For bottom jigging for rockfish, ling cod, red snapper and other heavy fish, a relatively short rod of medium stiffness is most appropriate. A one piece fiberglass rod of about five-and-a-half to six-and-a-half feet is quite inexpensive and works well.

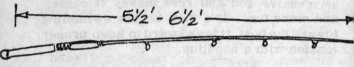

5½' - 6½'

MEDIUM STIFFNESS

Somewhat longer rods, to seven-and-a-half feet, are also good, but these are usually two piece and more expensive. Longer rods give more leverage in handling a fish if they are stiff enough. You can exert a strong steady force to lift big ones off the bottom. A longer flexible rod gives more shock absorbing action against hook tearing jerks by the fish. However, this shock absorbing action can absorb your leverage when trying to hold a fish off the bottom.

On the other hand, the shorter rod is much more convenient to handle in a small boat.

14

While rigging tackle or changing baits, you want to be able to rest the rod in the boat. If most of it is hanging over the side, it is difficult to reach the tip to grasp the line.

There is also the danger of knocking the whole outfit into the sea. I had this experience with one of my sons, then aged nine. He had just landed a lovely big sole and we were admiring it flopping in the bottom of our twelve-foot boat.

I dispatched it with a sharp blow on the head and bent down to dislodge the hooks. I heard a splash and felt a tug on the line leading from the hook. Looking up, I saw the line leading over the side and straight down into 100 feet of water.

The rod and reel had been resting across the gunwales and the boat had tipped somewhat as I bent over the fish. The whole outfit slid into the sea before I realized what was happening. A shorter rod would have been inside the boat.

Summing up on rods, I feel a short one piece fiberglass model is the best bet for most bottomfish. (A lighter flexible rod is more suitable for jigging for sole and other small flatfish.) These will be inexpensive and of satisfactory quality if purchased from a reputable dealer. Even the cheapest fiberglass rods will stand a lot of abuse.

The major differences between a quality rod and a cheap one are in the line guides, their wrappings, and in the reel seating arrangement.

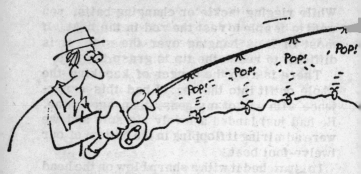

Cheap line guides will be made of light or brittle metal which tends to bend or break more easily with rough treatment. The wrappings which hold the line guides on the low priced rods tend to come unravelled.

Reel seats made of light metal can twist under pressure. Movable reel seats are supposed to have the advantage of adjusting the reel to the most convenient distance from

the butt. The problem with them is that they keep on adjusting while in use. The reels often twist sideways (out of line with the rod), rotate around the rod, or fall off altogether.

If you plan to fish for salmon as well as bottomfish, I would suggest a longer rod. It should be at least seven feet and preferably eight or eight-and-a-half feet long. It should have a sturdy butt and a soft, flexible tip. The sturdy butt section will give you the power to control a good sized fish and the flexible tip is advantageous as the shock absorber.

For heavy fish, you might want to employ Mr. Girling's technique of dropping the line down from a guide nearer the butt to give the effect of a short rod. (See page 109)

Choosing a Reel

My favorite reel is the center pin, single action type. It consists simply of a spool of line with handles, which revolves around a center pin mounted in a housing with an extending bracket for attaching to a rod.

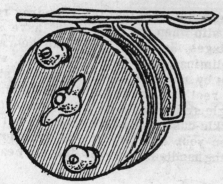

There is usually a rachet device to warn of a strike and provide that delightful zinging sound when the fish runs and pulls out line.

These reels are usually inexpensive and their simplicity makes them practically maintenance free. A little grease on the center pin and on the rachet pivot points is all that is needed to keep them trouble free for years of service.

Some people feel that the star-drag reels, which slip when the fish pulls, have some advantages. However, I don't like them at all. They eliminate the "feel" of the fish, which you get by manually controlling the single action reel with the palm of your hand.

Single action reels have the nick-name of "knuckle-dusters", since they can bark the skin on your knuckles if you grab for the whirling handles. However, it is very easy to

learn the proper technique, and a very thrilling sensation to feel the force of the running fish as the reel spins against your hand braking action. (My three young sons have been handling fish up to 50 pounds using these reels.)

Star drag reels do have a multiplying gear action which allows fast retrieve if a fish heads for the boat, but I have always been able to take up this slack successfully with my knuckle dusters.

Star drag reels allow you to just keep winding the handle while the action of the star drag (a slipping clutch arrangement) gives line to the fish when he pulls. You can actually be reeling in while the fish is

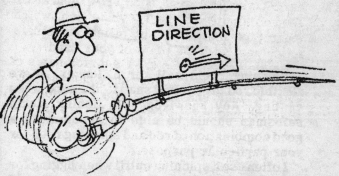

running out. While this automatic feature has some advantage for those who haven't learned the simple technique of controlling a single action reel, it can cause problems when landing a fish.

If a heavy fish keeps pulling when close to the boat, it is a strong temptation to tighten down on the drag. This allows you to pull harder without reel slip and haul the fish to the net or gaff. The fish, seeing the landing device, often makes one last dash for freedom and breaks the leader or tears out the hooks.

Spinning reels are the obvious choice for the caster. They allow long, tangle free casts and are relatively easy to learn to use. I would suggest a salt water model which is made to stand up in corrosive conditions. Salt water reels are also designed for heavier lines.

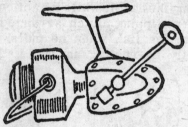

Spinning reels call for a longer, more flexible rod to give that snap to the lure when casting. Any knowledgeable fishing tackle salesman should be able to recommend a good combination of rod and spinning reel for your particular purpose.

I often use a spinning outfit when jigging for sole. It is a lightweight rod and small reel more suited to trout fishing, but it works well on the smaller flatfish. While I don't cast with it, the spinning reel allows the line to drop freely and quickly. The light, flexible rod shows nibbles on its sensitive tip and makes it easier to play the soft mouthed soles.

For surf-casting, a long, heavy, flexible rod and heavy duty casting or spinning reel is needed. The side cast reels, which rotate ninety degrees on the reel seat, are becoming very popular. Their large spools allow the use of heavier lines and the advantages of a spinning reel cast. Before winding in, the reel rotates to a position parallel with the rod. Now you can wind in with the positive control of a single action reel.

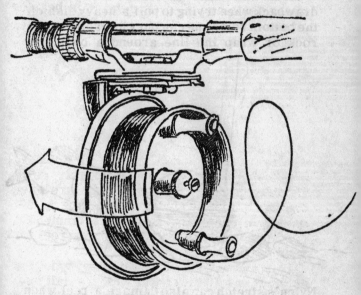

LINE

While some braided dacron or braided nylon lines are used for bottomfishing, the most popular is nylon monofilament. This type of line is inexpensive and is practically invisible underwater. Its smooth surface allows for easy casting and retrieving.

Nylon is an elastic material and will stretch under tension. This is both an advantage and disadvantage, depending on how you use it. A stretching line is obviously an advantage in absorbing shocks from a surging, jerking fish who might otherwise tear loose.

On the other hand, an elastic line can be a drawback when trying to pull a heavy fish off the bottom before he can bury himself under a rock or wrap the line around a boulder.

Nylon's stretch can also damage a reel when wound on too tightly.

If you reel in a large fish under a lot of pressure, the line will still be stretched as it wraps onto the drum of the reel. The same thing happens when you wind in a heavy load of kelp, other seaweed, or a snagged piece of wood or other debris.

22

After you have many turns of this tighly stretched line on the reel, a tremendous crushing force is exerted against the core and sides of the reel drum. Plastic reels will often split wide open under this pressure. (The pressure often doesn't crack the reel immediately, but many anglers have been startled to find a broken reel the next day).

Better quality reels, of metal or fibreglass reinforced plastic, will stand a great deal of line pressure, but even these will distort or twist slightly.

If you plan to do heavy fishing, it is a good idea to put several layers of a softer, braided line on the reel's core before adding the nylon. This will absorb a lot of the pressure.

However, the only certain method of preventing reel damage is to strip the line off again as soon as possible after winding it on under pressure. Then you can reel it in again without undue strain on it.

Some of the newer dacron braided lines will not stretch, but their opaque appearance is a drawback. Their rougher surface, caused by the braiding, increases line drag in the water.

LINE STRENGTH

Line strength is dependent on the size of the fish you are likely to catch. Casting or trolling requires different line from jigging or still fishing.

When casting or trolling, heavier lines have some disadvantages. Heavy casting lines, especially for spinning, tend to be too stiff for smooth pulling off the end of the spinning reel spool.

A limp nylon line is best for spinning. These also tend to be quite soft, which means they will nick and fray easily. Soft nylons also tend to crush in

knots, weakening the knot considerably. New technology nylons, however, combine a tough skin with limpness and more strength with the same thickness.

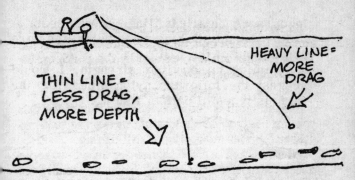

THIN LINE =
LESS DRAG,
MORE DEPTH

HEAVY LINE =
MORE
DRAG

When trolling, heavy lines increase friction drag and hold the lure nearer the surface. Since bottomfish are, by definition, on the bottom, this is undesirable. Slower trolling speed will overcome this problem to some extent.

Heavy lines are not a problem when jigging or stillfishing. There is not much line drag, unless fishing in a strong tidal current. Line is simply stripped off the reel until it hits bottom, so there are no casting problems.

Jigging for rockfish and ling cod is almost always over a rocky, often jagged bottom where it is very easy to snag the bottom. Heavy line is a real advantage in pulling loose from these hang-ups. You should use lighter

leaders, especially for ling cod who seem to be fussy about striking when bulky lines are coming out of the bait.

Summing up on line strength, I would suggest the following nylon lines for the various types of bottom fishing:

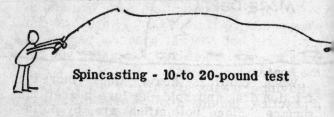

Spincasting - 10-to 20-pound test

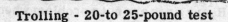

Trolling - 20-to 25-pound test

Jigging - 20-to 40-pound test

Lighter lines for jigging are good, but not necessary. I use my 20-pound test salmon lines for jigging because it is easy and convenient to use the same equipment. I just snap off my salmon lures and rig up for bottomfish.

It is much easier than carrying an extra rod and reel with heavier line. I probably lose a bit more gear by breaking lines when snagged on bottom, but it is not significant. However, I don't think I have lost any fish by using 20-pound test. (Many tyee salmon fishermen land 50-pound salmon on 20-pound test. Two of my teenaged sons have landed salmon over 53 pounds on single action reels and 20-pound line).

You should put at least 600 feet of line (two spools of 100 yards) on your reels if you plan to fish for large bottomfish. A big ling cod in a heavy tide can run out a lot of line. You can also strip out several hundred feet on a bottom hangup (when trolling) before you get the boat turned around.

Having extra line also allows you to follow a practice common among good fishermen everywhere. Before each outing, check the last ten feet of line for frays and nicks. Break off this portion and tie up your terminal gear to a fresh unfrayed end.

The end of the line also deteriorates right on the reel from exposure to sunlight. Many fishermen break off six to ten feet every few trips even if there is no sign of wear. When a line turns opaque and dull instead of shiny and translucent, it is time to break off this portion.

The entire line should be removed from the reel once a year and reversed. This will put the fresh, unused line from the core of the reel out on the working end. The end used all the previous season is now on the inside and seldom if ever comes off the reel.

WEIGHTS

Proper weight for bottom fishing is dependent on the fishing situation. No weight at all is the most effective rig for catching big perch under a dock or pier. Fishing in a heavy tide may require six to eight oz. when jigging or one pound or more when trolling.

The purpose of the weight is to get the line and lure down to the bottom where, hopefully, a hungry bottomfish is waiting. The size of weight required is dependent almost entirely on the forces retarding the line and lure from sinking.

If you drop a weight with no line connected, it plummets almost straight down. When you introduce the lure and line, these create a

28

friction drag which slows down the speed of descent. Add a tidal current moving sideways to the direction of descent and the situation is further complicated.

The tidal current pulls the line out horizontally proportionally to the force of the current. Thicker line and light bulky lures also increase drag. Fishing depth also affects friction drag since more line in the water means more friction surface.

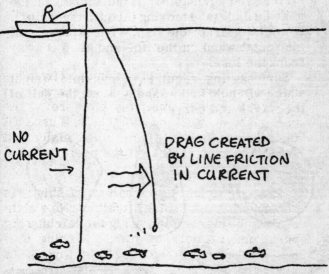

NO CURRENT

DRAG CREATED BY LINE FRICTION IN CURRENT

Generally speaking, three or four ounces is sufficient weight when jigging or drift fishing. In this type of fishing, the boat is moving in the same direction as the line and weight, so there is little if any line friction for the weight to overcome. If wind is blowing the boat to create a side drag on the line, add an extra ounce or two until the line goes down at a reasonable angle. Line angle should usually not exceed 45 degrees from vertical.

Spherical or tear drop weights are most efficient for jigging. Crescent shaped mooching sinkers work well, especially when drifting in a gentle current. Heavy currents may require a heavier round weight.

For trolling, there are many shapes of weights available. Slip sinkers, which can be set on the line away from the lure and trip on a strike, are advisable. If the sinker is too near the lure (and moving through the water), it might distract the fish. The sinker will also catch weed on the line and keep it away from the lure.

Surf casting requires a pyramid weight which will hold in the sand against the pull of the waves and currents.

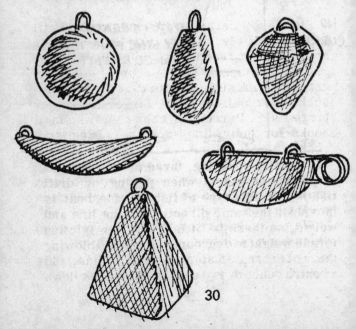

HOOKS

Buy good strong hooks of the proper size for the variety of fish you are seeking. Many makers, particularly English manufacturers, produce different grades of hooks. They will be labeled with such phrases as "Extra Strong", "Double Extra Strong", or even "Triple Extra Strong"!

Stainless steel hooks are excellent and will last indefinitely. If they are legal in your area, I would recommend using them.

Common sense is the best guide in choosing hook size. The basic rule is small hooks for small fish and larger hooks for large fish. Perch and sole require small hooks for their tiny mouths. Ling cod, rockfish, and halibut can swallow as big a hook as you can buy. Large hooks are also necessary when using live bait so the hook can hold the bait and still protrude enough to hook the fish.

We will suggest specific hook sizes when discussing each type of bottomfish.

One last comment on hooks. Keep them sharp! A darting fish will snatch a bait and dart away in a flash. Often he just brushes against the hook or it touches a hard bony part of his mouth.

A sharp hook will catch and dig in while a dull hook will merely slide off and you have missed your fish.

Salmon fishermen say that hooks should be "sticky sharp". This means that the points are so sharp they "stick" to any surface they touch. A good test is to put the point of the hook gently on your fingernail. If it sticks, your hook is sharp enough. Dull hooks will slide off.

Sharpen your hooks before baiting them when you start out on every fishing expedition. Carry a small sharpening stone or triangular file in your tackle box for this purpose.

Many anglers don't bother with hand filing since there are now battery operated hook sharpeners on the market which will produce a sticky sharp hook in seconds. Among them is one I developed, available at stores or from me for $19.95 plus tax and $4 handling at the address shown on page 3.

Don't try to shine up rusty hooks. Hooks are the least expensive part of your gear. Throw them away and use fresh ones.

SNAP SWIVEL

BARREL SWIVEL

THREE WAY SWIVEL

BEAD CHAIN SWIVEL

SWIVELS

You should use some type of swivel on any fishing line to prevent line twist between lure and the rod tip. Lures and weights tend to turn and roll as they are lowered or raised. They also turn and twist when drifting in the tidal current.

When you hook a fish, it is likely to roll and turn as you reel him in. Some fish will even twist themselves right around the line.

A swivel between leader and main line will eliminate most of this ravelling by turning with the leader and terminal tackle. The size of swivel should be proportional to the line strength and size of terminal gear.

Perch fishing requires a very tiny swivel so as not to scare off the very wary fish. Rockfish, ling cod and other large bottomfish call for a larger, stronger swivel.

Swivels are also used as connectors for such special rigs as paternoster booms. Three way swivels help separate gear for a number of rigs used for surf casting, bottom jigging, or even some live bait hookups.

33

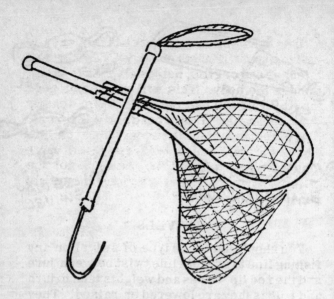

LANDING NETS AND GAFFS

Salmon fishermen prefer nets to land their catch. A large landing net provides a wide opening into which you can guide the thrashing, jerking salmon. Gaff hooks require more skill to get the salmon on the first try. If you miss a salmon with the gaff, he often lunges free or may even be knocked loose with the gaff.

Most bottomfish, on the other hand, tend to lie quietly on the water when brought to the surface. The rapid change in pressure from the deep water seems to take the life out of them, at least momentarily.

Rockfish and red snapper often have their air bladders so enlarged that they lie helplessly upside down or on their side with a bulging belly.

This behavior makes it relatively easy to gaff them and lift them aboard. Drive the gaff into the head or gills, being careful not to gaff them in the body. This will ruin some good meat. A gaff will tear out of flesh more easily than the tougher parts of head and gill covers.

It is best to aim for the underside of the jaw where the gaff can enter easily and catch inside the bony edge of the jaw or under the gills. Keep the gaff very sharp or it may not penetrate properly.

Landing nets are quite satisfactory for boating bottomfish, but can be a nuisance. Rockfish and ling cod tend to get badly tangled in the net and it is a tedious task to untangle the flapping, twisting fish. Rockfish spines and ling cod teeth will jam in the net mesh and are difficult to remove. It is also very easy to get a nasty wound from a rockfish spine puncture or from the sharp pointed teeth of a ling.

A small trout net is excellent for small bottomfish without too many spines. I find this a good method of landing sole, sand dab, and other small flatfish. A small net might also be good for perch, but most perch fishermen I know just pull the wriggling perch straight up onto the deck with the fishing line itself.

FISH BOX

It is desirable to have a place to store your catch on board. Fish flapping or sliding around on the deck will cause a mess and the slime will make the surface slippery.

When fishing for small sole, I often just use a big plastic bucket. However, this is not satisfactory for larger fish. There are many shapes and sizes of larger plastic containers available which make excellent fish boxes.

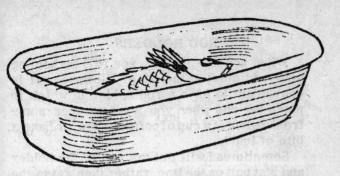

Baby bathtubs are perfect for all but the big ling cod. They are rectangular with rounded ends, are very sturdy and easy to keep clean. If you want a larger box, there are some small plastic boats available in the toy section of most department stores.

LOLLIPOP

You can also buy custom made fish boxes of galvanized iron or fiberglass. Fiberglass boxes are more expensive, but will last indefinitely. They also have rounded corners which are easier to clean than the square corners of galvanized boxes.

All fish boxes should be kept covered with a burlap sack, old towel, or other absorbent cloth soaked in sea water. This will keep the fish cool and moist until you get them to shore for cleaning.

ROD HOLDERS

When you are jigging, you will be holding your rod most of the time. However, it is convenient to have a rod holder in which to place the rod when you want to open some fresh bait, get a cup of coffee or tea, or have a bite of lunch.

Sometimes I will put my rod in the holder and just pull on the line, rather than raise the rod to get the jigging action. This takes only one hand and frees the other for holding a beverage cup.

When drifting for sole or rockfish, I have gotten many strikes when the rod was just sitting in the holder. The bait evidently just bounces near the bottom, turning in the tide to trigger a strike.

For trolling, rod holders are almost a necessity. It is very difficult to hold a rod by hand for a long period against the drag of the tackle. Propping the rod against an oarlock or jamming it into a crevice is very unsatisfactory. Furthermore, there is a big risk of accidentally knocking the whole outfit over the side.

You don't need expensive rod holders for bottomfish. Adjustable models are useful for trolling with bucktail flies and other special salmon fishing techniques, but have no advantage in bottomfishing.

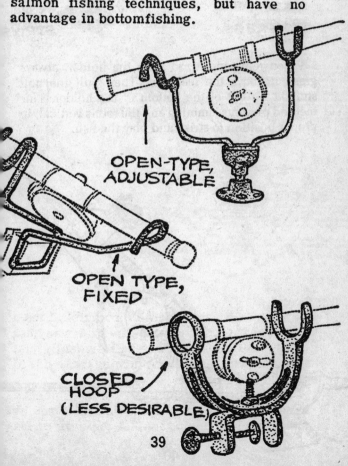

OPEN-TYPE, ADJUSTABLE

OPEN TYPE, FIXED

CLOSED-HOOP (LESS DESIRABLE)

TILT

SWIVEL

TEMPRESS

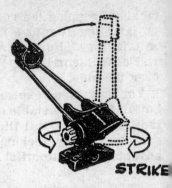

STRIKE

When removing a rod from the holder, always grasp it above the reel seat. Then pull the butt straight up out of the bottom of the holder. This method prevents jamming and the rod is vertical, in proper position to strike and play the fish.

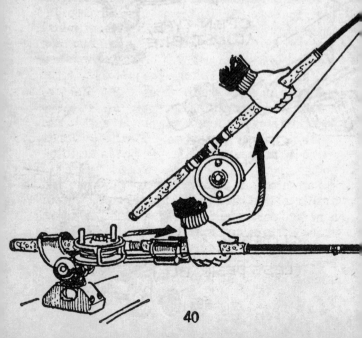

CHAPTER II
BAITS

Most bottomfishing is done with natural bait, but artificial lures are finding increasing acceptance. Various types of metal jigs from Scandanavian countries and feather jigs and plastic or rubber lures from Japan are used more and more frequently.

In the special section on reef fishing, author Sidney Girling describes his success with homemade rubber octopus lures. In his opinion, properly designed artificial lures will outfish natural bait for rockfish and ling cod.

Sometimes a combination of natural and artificial bait is effective. A narrow strip of herring, pork rind, a strip of fish belly, or even a strip of cod skin can be hooked to the end of an artificial lure. This bit of natural food dangling on the end of a moving lure will often trigger a strike.

41

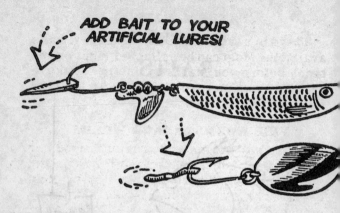

ADD BAIT TO YOUR ARTIFICIAL LURES!

In experiments with our underwater research camera, we found that artificial-natural bait combinations were very effective for bottomfish. The productivity of jigging lures was more than doubled when we added bait to the hooks.

Sole, sanddabs, and sculpins would be attracted to the flopping, flashing lure but were hesitant to strike until it momentarily stopped moving. With bait they snatched at the hook more readily than with just the bare wire.

Jigging lures with spinner tails were extremely effective. The vibrating spinner focussed the strike on the bait and hook.

NATURAL BAIT

There is a wide selection of natural baits available. Most can be collected right on the beach before you start out fishing. Take a suitable container so the bait can be kept fresh and alive if possible.

PILE WORMS or SAND WORMS

These sea worms are a natural food for most bottomfish, but especially for flounder, sole, and perch. There is even a story of an old timer who caught big chinook salmon by mooching with pile worms.

They resemble a centipede with many legs. They vary in color from green to brown. They are quite firm and juicy and make an excellent bait. In fact, if I had to choose one single bait for bottomfishing, I would pick the pileworm.

They can be found between and under the clusters of barnacles and mussels on rocks, docks, or pilings. You can also find them under rocks or waterlogged pieces of driftwood. You can dig for them in the mud, gravel, or sand in the lower half of the intertidal zone. You will often find pile worms when digging for clams. (See Heritage House book, *How to Catch Shellfish*.)

Other varieties of sea-worms, called tube-worms, live inside a thin cylindrical shell. They will be found sticking out from the mussels and barnacles on floating docks and can be gathered at any stage of the tide.

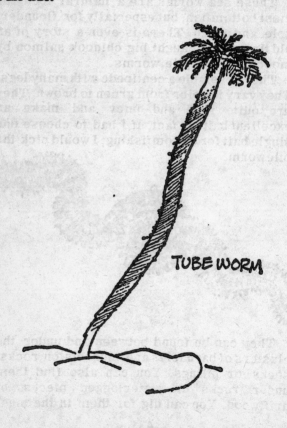

TUBE WORM

KEEPING PILEWORMS ALIVE

Pileworms keep much better in cool weather and should be kept out of the sun. If you plan to use them the same day, put them in a small box, plastic container, or bucket with a quantity of sand or fine beach gravel.

You can keep them alive for several days by cleaning off all clinging mud or sand and wrapping carefully in dry newspaper. Store in a cool, dry place.

HOOKING PILEWORMS

Pileworms can be threaded on the hook right up to the eye (of the hook) with an inch or two left to wiggle off the point. If worms are scarce or if you are fishing for small sole, small chunks of worm on the tip of the hook work well.

CLAMS

Pieces of any variety of clam make very good bait, especially for flatfish. The tougher neck sections of cockles, horse clams, and large butter clams are better than the tender parts since they stay well on the hook.

Keep clams fresh by storing them without water, but covered with a moist cloth. Clams crowded in a small container of water will soon suffocate.

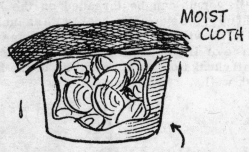

MOIST CLOTH

KEEP WATER (ESPECIALLY RAIN WATER) FROM COLLECTING IN CONTAINER.

MUSSELS

Mussels can be used whole or broken into pieces for small fish. If you break up a mussel, leave bits of shell attached to the meat for a more natural looking bait.

Whole mussels should be removed from the shell, then turned inside out and placed on the hook. This will allow it to "milk" into the surrounding water and attract the fish.

Open mussels by putting a knife blade between the tips of the shell and cutting to the hinge. They are difficult to keep on the hook, but threading the hook through a bit of shell or the toughest part of the meat will help. If you want to be fussy, you might even try holding it on by wrapping with fine thread. Mussels will be found in abundance clinging to rocks, pilings and floating docks.

SHRIMP AND PRAWNS

If you have a shrimp trap, you can save some of your catch for bottomfishing. Shrimp can also be found at low tide along the shore and against and under rocks and seaweed.

Live shrimp are very good bait, but should be used immediately as they do not keep well. I have kept them alive in cool weather (March) in large plastic garbage cans by changing the water every morning and evening. However, they die quickly in warm summer weather.

Shrimp and prawns can be hooked through the tail or through the back as shown.

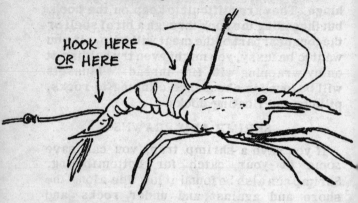

HOOK HERE OR HERE

Shrimp tails are good bait, but it is difficult to hold the soft meat on the hook. Leave the shell on and thread carefully to avoid breaking the slight bond between meat and shell.

GHOST SHRIMP

Ghost shrimp are the very soft, pale, creatures found in the mud and sand when digging for clams. They make long oval shaped holes as they burrow through the sand, mud or gravel.

They can be fished in a similar manner to shrimp or prawns, or they can be broken in chunks and threaded on a hook.

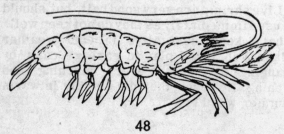

SHORE CRABS

Small shore crabs are very abundant under rocks, seaweed, and almost any hiding place which is dark and moist. The soft shelled crabs make the best bait.

All crabs grow by shedding their shells periodically and swelling up to a new larger size. Just after the old shell is discarded, the crab is very soft and a tasty morsel for most bottomfish. Thread them whole on the hook.

Crabs will keep in a bucket for several days if covered with a moist cloth.

LIMPETS AND WHELKS

Limpets are easily obtainable on any rocky or gravel beach. They will be found clinging to rocks or seawalls right up to the high tide level. They should be gathered with a quick motion, slipping a knife between the single shell and the rock. If the limpet is alerted to your presence, he will grab the rock firmly and be much more difficult to remove.

Whelks are found near low tide level and can be used like a limpet after removal from the shell.

WHELK

HERRING

Herring is the one natural bait that you can easily obtain from tackle shops or live bait dealers. Frozen herring and herring strip can be used whole or in chunks. When I try bottomfishing after an early morning salmon trip, my left-over herring is usually my only bait.

Herring can be mooched or trolled, either whole or plug-cut, to catch rockfish and ling cod. Mooched herring is also used for halibut. A number of lucky anglers have landed huge halibut while mooching for salmon over sandy bottoms.

PLUG·CUT RIG:

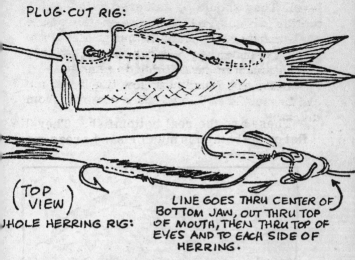

(TOP VIEW)

HOLE HERRING RIG:

LINE GOES THRU CENTER OF BOTTOM JAW, OUT THRU TOP OF MOUTH, THEN THRU TOP OF EYES AND TO EACH SIDE OF HERRING.

LIVE HERRING RIG:
PUT HOOK & LINE THROUGH JAWS FROM BELOW.

HOOK JUST UNDER SKIN BEHIND DORSAL FIN. PUTTING HOOK TOO LOW CAN PARALYSE OR KILL HERRING.

Live herring is a deadly bait for rockfish and lings. They just can't resist a live herring wriggling on a hook. Shiner perch and other small fish are also used alive in the same manner.

Herring and other baitfish can be kept alive in a large plastic garbage can if the water is changed frequently. Minnow or bait buckets which float in the water next to the boat can also be used.

51

CHAPTER III
SOLE & FLOUNDER

These are the real bottomfish. They lie flat on the bottom in mud or sand areas most of their lives.

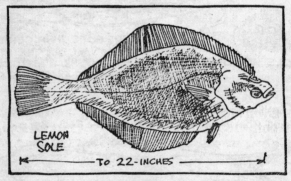

LEMON SOLE

TO 22-INCHES

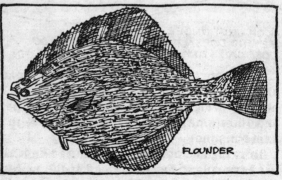

FLOUNDER

These flatfish are a dramatic example of how nature adapts a species for survival. Evidence shows that these fish are descended from a more normal upright shaped fish (like a Perch or fresh-water Sunfish).

Certain fish found that by lying flat in the mud or sand they were able to hide from enemies and lie in wait for their own food. An evolutionary process gradually changed the shape and position of certain fins and -- most dramatic of all -- one eye actually migrated to the other side of the head!

Even today all flatfish begin life with eyes on both sides of the body. At a very early age, one eye moves to the other side of the head so he can lie flat in the sand with both eyes on the "top" side!

They also developed a remarkable ability to camouflage themselves. I have watched (in the Undersea Gardens) a Sole swim to a sandy spot, settle to the bottom, then cover most of his body with a thin sand layer by two quick flips of his fins!

CATCHING FLATFISH

These habits are an important key to catching Sole and Flounder. Since they like to lie hidden in the sand waiting for their food, you have to get the bait in exactly the right spot to catch them. The best way to find a good Sole bed is to ask lots of questions locally. Most good sole fishermen have definite "marks" to line up the best spot.

Try to find out these precise directions rather than a general "over on that side of the bay" which still leaves you to do a lot of groping to find the spot. Knowing how to use "markers" is important in following directions, or in identifying locations you discover yourself.

LINE UP TWO PAIRS OF PERMANENT OBJECTS.

THE CLOSER TO A 90° ANGLE BETWEEN PAIRS, THE BETTER.

90°

Some Sole beds are in the middle of large bays and are very difficult to locate. There is an excellent Sole bed in Patricia Bay in front of my home near Sidney. An old time fisherman showed me how to find it, using Navy anchoring buoys to line up the spot.

We woke up one morning to find the buoys had been moved over a mile to a different mooring area. It took most of the next season to relocate this very productive spot!

HEH! I'LL BET THEY STILL THINK IT WAS THE NAVY MOVED THOSE BUOYS!

Sole and Flounder beds can also be located by studying marine charts. Look for a mud bottom (or sand if mud bottom is not available) with a very gradual slope. A gradual slope is indicated by wide distances between depth graduation lines. They can be found at almost any depth from ten to fifteen feet to 150 feet or more.

Contrary to popular belief, flatfish prefer a mud bottom to a sand bottom. More tiny food organisms feed on the nutrients found in mud than in more sterile and barren sand.

These tiny organisms are eaten by larger organisms, starting the food chain which supports fish life. Fisheries Department data shows that heaviest concentrations of flatfish are found on mud bottoms.

Good Sole beds can be very productive indeed!

BAITING THE HOOK

There are two schools of thought on this subject. Some people feel that the worm or other bait should be threaded on the hook to cover it completely and hide it from the fish. Others feel that the hook should be put lightly through the worm so that it can wriggle freely. My own preference when fishing Flounder and Sole is to thread small chunks of worm right onto the hook covering the point and barb. All fish strike from instinct and not by rational thought. If they see or smell natural food, they will grab it no matter how it is hooked. Threading on small chunks saves scarce bait!

Hook size should not be too large for these small-mouthed fishes. A No. 2 to No. 4 can be used in most cases and a No. 1 for large Flounder. The illustrations from here to page 60 show rigs for Sole and Flounder, but as mentioned, multiple-hook rigs are illegal in B.C. and some other Pacific Coast waters. Check applicable Provincial or State regulations before you go fishing.

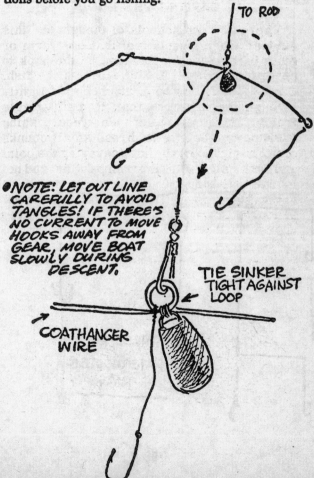

TO ROD

●NOTE: LET OUT LINE CAREFULLY TO AVOID TANGLES! IF THERE'S NO CURRENT TO MOVE HOOKS AWAY FROM GEAR, MOVE BOAT SLOWLY DURING DESCENT.

TIE SINKER TIGHT AGAINST LOOP

COATHANGER WIRE

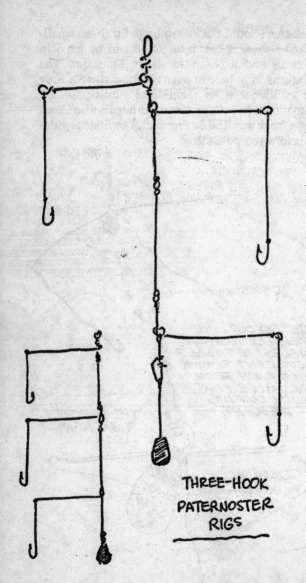

THREE-HOOK
PATERNOSTER
RIGS

LEGER RIGS

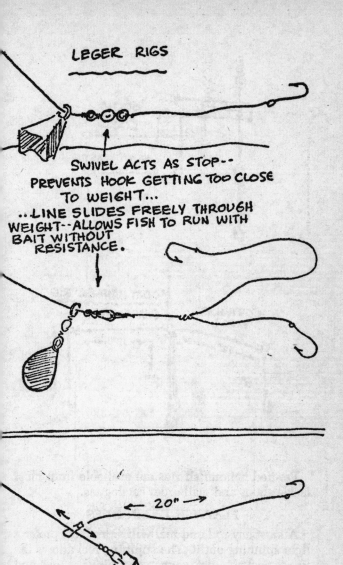

SWIVEL ACTS AS STOP--
PREVENTS HOOK GETTING TOO CLOSE
TO WEIGHT...
...LINE SLIDES FREELY THROUGH
WEIGHT--ALLOWS FISH TO RUN WITH
BAIT WITHOUT
RESISTANCE.

← 20" →

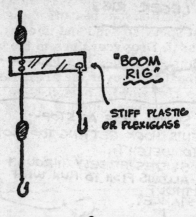

"BOOM RIG"

STIFF PLASTIC OR PLEXIGLASS

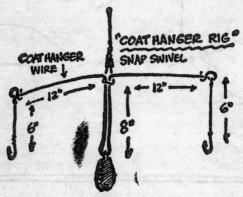

"COAT HANGER RIG"
SNAP SWIVEL

COAT HANGER WIRE ↓

12"   12"

6"   8"   6"

Pre-tied bottomfish rigs are available from most tackle shops and mail order catalogues.

FLATFISH TECHNIQUES

Almost any rod and reel will work but I prefer a light spinning outfit. The spinning reel allows the line to peel off quickly when dropping the line, and the light rod and line gives sporty action when landing fish.

To start fishing, note the direction of wind and tide. Position your boat off to the side of your "hot spot" so wind and tide will carry you across it. Drop your lines to the bottom, then pull up six inches to a foot.

As the boat drifts over the area, raise and lower the rod slowly, bumping the bottom every few feet. You should get lots of active, sharp tugs as the flatfish grabs the bait. Set

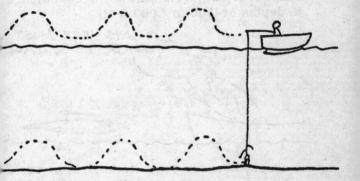

the hook with a short jerk, then reel him in!

Small fish can be lifted aboard, but a small trout net is a good idea for larger specimens. Kill them with a sharp blow on the head, then store them in a cool, shady place. A picnic cooler, or even a large bucket with a damp cloth over the top, will keep the fish firm and fresh.

Most of my personal experience with flatfish has been in deep water (over 100 feet) and I have found that a calm day at slack tide is most productive. If there is much wind or a strong tide, the boat moves too fast over the Sole bed and it is difficult to keep the bait on the bottom. In shallower areas, you can anchor over the spot and have good fishing in any reasonable weather or tide. Commercial net fishermen report best success with flatfish at slack water conditions.

DEPTHS FOR FINDING FLATFISH

Sole and flounders can be found in a wide range of depths, from just under the surface to depths of 1500 or 2000 feet!

Starry flounder often lie in shallow water off sandy shorelines. When trolling for cohoes in shallow water in early fall, I have often noticed flounder scurry away from the approaching boat. When drifting over shallow sand bars looking for crabs, we have been startled by the sudden cloud of sand and mud as a big flounder rushes off from practically under the boat.

Flatfish will often work their way in with a flooding tide, feeding on small crabs and

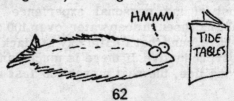

other organisms very close to the water's edge. They work their way back out with the ebbing tide.

Flatfish tend to gather in groups over areas rich in nutrients and feed. These can be found at almost any depth, but 50 to 125 feet is probably a good depth range to work.

Generally speaking, the larger flatfish are in slightly deeper water than the smaller varieties. Some predatory species, like the big Petrale sole move around in search of small fish. I have caught them over six pounds in the midst of a school of small sand dabs.

All sole and flounder migrate to deeper water to spawn. They often begin moving down after the first fall storms in October or November. They spawn in late winter or early spring in deep water, then return to shallower water in April or May.

TROLLING FOR FLOUNDER

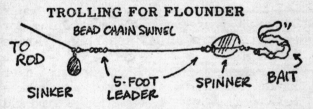

Large flounder can also be taken by a very slow troll or by motor mooching. A spinner and sea worm combination is the preferred bait. Strips of herring or other fish flesh are also effective.

Some of the rigs used for trout will work for flounder, but the multiple spinner "Willow-leaf" or "Gang-troll" arrangements offer too much drag and keep the line too shallow.

The bait should be very close to the bottom to get flounder. Slow rowing is an excellent way to troll, giving an erratic action to the lure as the boat moves ahead with each stroke.

Trolling with the motor in reverse will give a slower speed than in forward gear as the boat moves against the resistance of the square stern.

Putting the motor in and out of gear is another method of slowing the trolling speed.

On some occasions, flounder will move up to mid-water areas to chase herring schools.

Some fishermen get good catches of flounder off the central Oregon coast trolling well off the bottom with whole herring or herring strip. Some are caught while trolling for salmon.

CHAPTER IV
HALIBUT

These are the largest of the flatfish and many people consider them the best eating fish in the sea! They grow to enormous size -- sports fishermen take many specimens over 100 pounds each year. Exceptional giants can exceed 200 pounds.

Halibut are tricky fish to catch. Generally speaking, they are found on large, flat, sand or mud banks off the open coast and in Juan de Fuca Strait. They can be found in shallow inlets or hundreds of feet down offshore.

Halibut are often found on the top of shallow banks surrounded by much deeper water. Halibut prefer a sand or mud bottom, but inhabit these shallow reefs even if they are rocky.

Fisheries department personnel working on the Bowie Sea Mount near the Queen Charlotte Islands jigged for halibut on this rocky undersea mountain using chromed lead Norwegian cod jigs. They were quite successful, getting fish up to 200 lbs.

In Southeast Alaska, huge halibut move into estuary areas off the rivermouths when the salmon gather to spawn. Evidently they catch and eat whole salmon, particularly pinks and sockeye. To these monsters, reputed to weigh as much as 500 pounds, even a ten pound salmon is just a tasty tidbit.

Speaking of Alaska, there is a sign on the dock at the Alaskan capital city of Juneau which warns boaters not to bring large halibut aboard small boats. There have been a number of accidents when large halibut, apparently played out, were dragged into small wooden boats.

The halibut would suddenly thrash around and bang his powerful body and tail against the bottom and sides of the boat. Several boats have had hull planking smashed open, and the boats have gone down with loss of life. The recommended procedure is to hook the fish to a strong towline with a heavy rubber shock absorber and tow it slowly to shore.

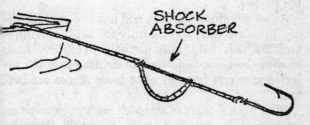

SHOCK ABSORBER

If you still want to try for halibut after that story, get some heavy salmon tackle and at least 1000 to 1500 feet of heavy nylon line (perhaps 40 pound test).

Halibut are carnivirous predators and will eat any live fish -- herring, perch, rockfish, cod. Rig them alive on a large hook (see ling cod section) and drift over the halibut

grounds with the bait just off the bottom. Let the weight hit bottom frequently to be sure you are deep enough.

Halibut will also take many kinds of frozen bait. Commercial halibut fishermen use pieces of squid, octopus, herring and true cod for bait on their set lines. Mooched whole herring or plug-cut herring are also very effective. Some anglers troll very slowly with the herring about three feet behind a big flasher.

As we mentioned earlier, cod jigs and other artificial lures are used successfully for halibut. All jigging methods, using both natural and artificial bait, employ the basic technique of drifting over the selected area and bouncing the lures across the bottom.

After several years of research with our underwater camera we were finally able to get the first ever pictures of halibut striking lures. They shied away from jigs more than two feet above the bottom. But when we jigged with the lure actually touching the bottom, they attacked aggressively and inhaled the lure with a sucking motion. (The lure disappeared in less than one-tenth of a second!) We show this exciting footage in our seminars and videos.

CHAPTER V

ROCKFISH

TYPICAL ROCKFISH

There are at least fifteen different varieties of Rockfish (often called Rock-cod) along the North Pacific Coast. They have an air bladder which allows them to hang motionless in the water a few feet above a rocky bottom.

They will attack any shiny lure, feather jig, or natural herring bait which is dragged past them. While they will also feed on clams, pile worms, etc., it is easier to attract them with a slow moving, shiny bait or lure.

Most Rockfish tend to hang in schools in

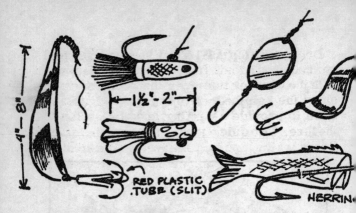

RED PLASTIC TUBE (SLIT)

HERRIN

one rocky area and will not venture far in search of food. The Black Rockfish and Yellow-tailed Rockfish (sometimes called "Sea Bass") are exceptions to this rule. They are roving, mid-water fish who cover wide areas in search of food.

These active, sporty fish will strike trolled lures readily and many have been taken on bucktail flies. If you happen on a school of these fish, you can have great sport if you stop your boat and cast small lures into the school. They will strike aggressively and put up a strong fight. In many ways they look and fight like freshwater bass.

A very effective method of catching the bottom dwelling varieties of Rockfish is to drift slowly over a rocky bottom. Most productive areas are often near reefs or along rocky shorelines.

They often gather in large schools around underwater features such as shipwrecks, junked cars, rocks and reefs. Many people catch them casting from breakwaters.

Along the edge of kelp beds (or even right in them) is also productive.

70

Drop your line until it hits bottom, then pull up about 5 or 6 feet. Let your boat drift slowly with the wind, or tide over the rocky area or along the kelp bed. Work your rod up and down to provide a darting, erratic action to the lure. Two quick jerks, followed by slack line to let the lure flutter down is a procedure used by many commercial cod fishermen.

The key to providing proper action is to have sharp, erratic jerks to attract the fish, then the slower flutter (or even hanging still momentarily) to allow the fish to grab it.

Every minute or two, you should let out line until it hits bottom, then re-position it 5 or 6 feet up. This will keep you near the bottom as you drift over areas of varying depth. You will probably find one spot in your drift where you get most of your strikes. If this is the case, keep making short drifts over this area or anchor just on the uptide side and let your lure drift into the productive spot.

Another method for catching **Black Rockfish** is used by our artist , Nelson Dewey, who learned from an experienced fisherman friend. (A good way to learn any type of fishing is by asking the local experts who are usually more than willing to share their knowledge!)

Towards evening, he rows his dinghy into a partially sheltered bay with a good tidal flow. By rowing against the current and slightly faster, he "trolls" a line through the back eddies where the fish seem to congregate to feed. He uses small feathered plugs with little or no weight.

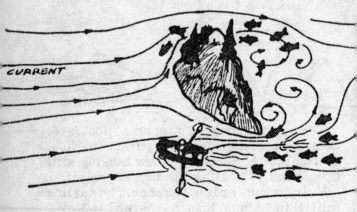

CURRENT

At dusk the fish will often come to the surface (apparently to feed) and will jump! In the semi-darkness, it's difficult to see them, but a weightless lure trolled six to ten feet behind the boat, just below the surface, will usually bring a good catch.

(Note: be sure to have a good flashlight to find your way back to shore and to warn off other boats!)

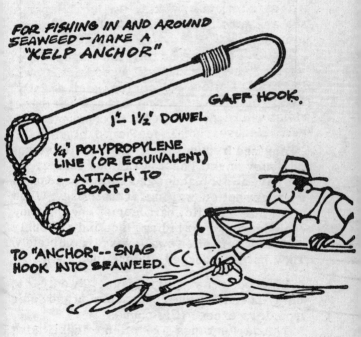

FOR FISHING IN AND AROUND
SEAWEED — MAKE A
"KELP ANCHOR"

GAFF HOOK.

1" - 1½" DOWEL

¼" POLYPROPYLENE
LINE (OR EQUIVALENT)
-- ATTACH TO
BOAT.

TO "ANCHOR" -- SNAG
HOOK INTO SEAWEED.

CHAPTER VI

LINGCOD

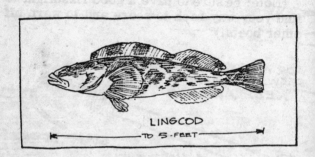

LINGCOD
TO 5 FEET

Ling cod frequent rocky areas with strong tidal movement. These voracious feeders do not have an air bladder and lie motionless on the rocky bottom waiting for their prey. When a darting erratic bait comes near, they explode from their hiding place and viciously attack the bait, often swallowing it completely. They put up a dogged, determined fight.

Lingcod grow quite large. Twenty- to thirty-pound fish are not uncommon and some monsters exceed fifty pounds.

The large Lings are often caught using Rockfish for bait! Sometimes when playing a Rockfish (or Sole or Flounder) the line will suddenly stop jerking and you feel only a heavy pull on the line. If you haven't snagged the bottom or some kelp, a large Lingcod has probably grabbed hold of your Rockfish!

You can bring both fish to the boat with a firm steady reeling of line. When they are close to the boat, do not lift the fish partially out of the water or the Ling will let go. If you

quietly slip a net under them, or gaff the Ling (the Rockfish is already hooked), you will have two fish, the Ling probably a large specimen.

If you want to catch large Ling, use a live Rockfish or Sole for bait. Rig two of the largest hooks you have, one through the snout and the other through the side back at the anal fin.

NOTE: CHECK LOCAL REGULATIONS FOR POSSIBLE CLOSED SEASONS ON LINGCOD....

Let the fish swim freely and he will head straight for the bottom. Keep him just off the rocks by raising and lowering the rod. This will keep him from hiding in a crevice. Use only about two to four ounces of weight (or none at all if it is not too deep).

CHAPTER VII

RED SNAPPER

RED SNAPPER

This member of the Rockfish family lives at greater depths than any of his relatives. They are seldom caught less than 60 or 70 feet deep, and commercial catches are made at 600 to 700 feet down in offshore areas!

Red Snapper can be taken on the same type of lure as other Rockfish. Any shiny lure, feather jig, or herring bait will bring a solid strike if bounced within the sight of a hungry snapper — and it seems they are always hungry!

They have very large mouths, so you might experiment with larger baits to see if this method will catch larger fish. (As we explain in our book, *How to Catch Salmon: Basic Fundamentals*, Federal Fisheries Department experiments showed that large lures caught the biggest chinook salmon.)

When you bring up a Snapper from deep water, his air bladder will be puffed up so large that the whole fish is bloated. The air bladder will often push some of the internal organs right up into the fish's mouth!

Snapper can grow quite large. Twenty pounders are not uncommon. They are delicious eating. Some people claim the white flaky meat tastes similar to crab!

Fishing Notes

GIRLING ON BOTTOMFISHING

The following special section deals with fishing rockfish and ling cod off the reefs near Victoria. It is a remarkable story, written by a remarkable gentleman, the late Sidney Girling. He fished these reefs from a rowboat until he was 85.

His theories on vertical jigging with lures designed especially for this purpose have proven extremely effective as he outlines in his excellent article. The serious bottomfish devotee will find his material absorbing and very valuable. Newcomers to bottomfishing will find his methods simple and effective.

Although some of the material is now dated, it is still generally applicable and his octopus lure design has stood the test of time. His historical background is interesting and everyone will be delighted to read his philosophy of fishing and his comments on fishing with children.

CHAPTER VIII
FISHING THE REEFS FOR ROCKFISH AND LING COD

By Sidney S. Girling

There must be many people living on our extensive rocky coastline -- and boaters on cruising craft with rockfish actually under their doorstep -- who would be glad to supplement their food supply with excellent fresh fish at short notice and little cost.

But first, why rockfish? Why not salmon? In fact, why go fishing at all? One is bound to go shopping sometime and there are plenty of good fish in the stores.

Why take all that trouble painting the boat, fixing the tackle, rowing to the reef, catching the slimy, spiny creatures, filleting and disposing of the remains when any commercial fisherman will gladly do all this for you?

Yes, it could be said of most hobbies that the material product of our labor could be much more easily obtained in the stores. Possibly the reason some of us enjoy our hobbies and the work they entail is that the urge to engage in such productive activities is as much a part of us as our hands and brains. We are satisfying an inner compulsion that for over two million years was partly responsible for our survival.

Throughout the greater part of that vast stretch of time, those defective individuals who lacked that urge and lay abed dreaming the happy hours away may have had offspring but they were less likely to survive to perpetuate this deficiency of their parents. So it came about that this subconscious desire became part of our makeup.

However, very late in that two million years, when civilization was invented, some perceptive individuals managed to survive very well indeed by inducing others to do the physical work for them. It appears they may

have left descendants who do not get emotional satisfaction when engaged in such productive occupations as handicrafts, gardening, etc. In fact they look upon them as chores.

But there are still, in these days of highrise apartments and supermarkets, many fortunate people who have, and are in a position to satisfy, that inborn instinct to produce at least some small part of their physical needs by their own efforts. Such

endeavor is good for the soul. It may be cooking, dressmaking, gardening, wine making, beekeeping, hunting, fishing, tackle making, artistry or handicrafts of various kinds.

The material products of these activities can be purchased in the supermarkets but the spiritual satisfaction derived from one's own achievement cannot be bought anywhere, at any price.

In past years I have engaged in all of these occupations except dressmaking but the present writing is about rockfishing, which I have found to be most beneficial, physically and emotionally. And compared to salmon fishing -- more consistently profitable. The end product is more palatable to many people. For those fortunate anglers who have learned to use their hands, making tackle and lures gives them these benefits plus a financial gain.

With many hobbies there are operations essential to completion of the project one would gladly skip. In this case, filleting the fish and disposal of the remains. However a determination to do it yourself, not leaving the unpleasant work to others, is good for the psyche.

If the following writing seems to downgrade salmon and salmon fishing, it is to awaken saltwater anglers to the merits of reef fishing once you have lures as clean and efficient as those used in salmon fishing.

As food, many salmon fishermen say they prefer fresh caught rockfish or ling cod to salmon. My wife and I agree, but I repeat, fresh caught! Even a few days delay makes a difference. Cold storage gives us good sustenance but the fine flavor is lost; sometimes a new one acquired. Bought fillets are never as good as fresh caught, unless of course the bought fillets are fresh caught.

To make sure, catch the fish yourself or get your youngsters to get them for you. Once you get to know where, how and when, a catch is fairly certain.

BOTTOMFISH
HERE:
8:15 AM TUES
8:50 AM WED
9:25 AM THUR.

This cannot be said of salmon even if you get out of your warm bed before dawn, that unearthly hour which is the best time to get good salmon and prove you have intestinal fortitude.

I have done this and had good fishing, but at my age prefer to be out in the warm sunshine after a good meal. Those lovely calm sunny days are not the best days for salmon fishing.

The female of the species instinctively expects the male to return from the hunt with something for the family to eat. Usually she is not too concerned about the sporting angle.

The following incident is recalled because it appears to show that the subconscious feelings, implanted in us before civilization came into being, still influence our reactions.

It was, I believe, in the summer of 1953, one of those lovely Victoria days of clear sky, bright sunshine and no wind, that my wife and I went fishing from Brentwood Bay on the Saanich Inlet. We fished around Senanus Island getting rockfish and soles, then lastly a large flounder near the boathouse on our way back.

As we unloaded the fish on to the float, two ladies from a fishing party that had pulled in ahead of us, stopped to look at the fish. I heard one say, "The boys said there were no fish in the Inlet."

...THOSE LOOK LIKE FISH, TO ME...

I shall never forget those words and the way in which she said them, somewhat as if the fish we had were just as acceptable to her as the fish the "boys" said were not there. There were plenty of good fish in the Inlet but not the kind they were fishing for.

Now in my 88th year I feel an enjoyable part of my life would be wasted if I did not pass on to others the knowledge acquired

during many years of fishing experience, from sticklebacks from a pond in Essex, England, 1899, to a 49-lb. ling cod, 1969, and bigger fish that got away.

Through the Thirties I landed many rockfish and lingcod, casting from the shore, using wooden plugs, (homemade from cedar boughs), because plug casualties were high and it is fun to make your own.

To reach the fish, the plug must move near the bottom, so it is quite likely to get snagged. A spincasting outfit is not strong enough to pull free, so it is better to use a stiffer casting rod with a free spool casting reel and 15-lb. nylon at least.

The most productive fishing was from the Victoria breakwater during late winter when the kelp has disappeared, and spring, before the kelp shows, starting an hour after sunset and continuing into the night. We often stayed until ten o'clock. The fish, black rockfish (commonly called black bass), feed on the surface after dark, travelling in schools along the shoreline, occasionally splashing. It was rarely we came away empty handed.

If, some calm evening, standing on a rocky shore in the near dark, you hear an occasional splash, it is most likely the black rockfish feeding. They do not bite in rough or phosphorescent water.

We found the most effective lure to be a strip of fresh pork rind, the thinner the better, salted to preserve and whiten it, then cut to resemble a small fish about two and a half inches long. Punch a hole in the head end with the point of a sharp knife and hang on a 1-0 hook, free to wiggle, with one-third ounce of lead clamped on the nylon about 8 inches from the hook. More weight will sink the lure too deep.

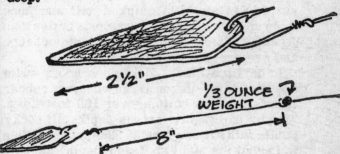

2½"

⅓ OUNCE WEIGHT

8"

This bait, cast out about 70 feet and retrieved while jerking the rod tip occasionally, is very effective. The bait is so tough one piece will land many fish, and spares kept in a jar with wet salt will keep for years (twenty to my knowledge) and still take fish.

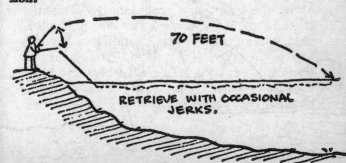

70 FEET

RETRIEVE WITH OCCASIONAL JERKS.

There being no spincasting reels in the Thirties and since a free spool reel will not cast one-third ounce, we cast with no reel, dropping the line at our feet. A spincasting outfit would be much better.

The fish may also be taken after dark, fly fishing with a white streamer fly. This can be done from a wharf, boat or rocky point.

We usually landed more than could be eaten fresh, so having no fridge, dressed the surplus fillets with smoked salt and hung them up to dry. This to my taste is better than freezing. Smoked fillets make a nice change and are excellent for fish cakes.

In daytime black rockfish schools swim deeper. I have taken large ones, on rubber lures, from the bottom, over 100 feet down. Also by trolling at various depths off rocky points with salmon lures. The problem then is to find the right spot and depth, as with salmon, with one difference. If you note tide conditions when you get one, you will likely find them near the same spot and depth day after day. When the tide turns they will likely be on the other side of the point.

We all know getting salmon is a game of chance. Possibly that is one reason it is so popular, like gambling. If you are lucky the reward may be big. With experience, you may increase your chances of success, but you can never approach the degree of certainty attainable when fishing for rockfish.

Salmon are rovers -- here today, gone tomorrow -- feeding in unpredictable areas, depths and times. On the contrary, with fish living on the reefs, you know if there are fish there, they are there all day and every day, provided they are not fished out. True, lingcod move to shallower water to spawn but they are back to deep water and their lairs before March.

Not only are bottom fish a source of excellent food, they also provide dependable outdoor entertainment. There are a great variety of fish species. From an area of not more than four city blocks I have taken in recent years six species of rockfish: copper, quillback, black, orange, red snapper and vermilion, also ling cod, cabezon, marbled sculpin, dogfish, kelp greenling, white spotted greenling, rock, sand and flathead soles. All were caught on vertically operated rubber lures and all edible. I lost a fish that took off with speed into deeper water. It felt like a streetcar, but was likely a large halibut. I kept tightening the brake but there was no stopping it. After many yards of line had run out, the 20 lb. nylon broke.

The behavior of bottom fish is very different from that of salmon. A ling cod, from small to ten pounds or so will fight to get free, but a large one makes no attempt to run. They appear somewhat insensitive to pain or fear.

Frequently I've hooked a rockfish around three pounds weight, 100 feet down, more or less, and in a few seconds there is a dead stop to raising the fish. You wonder if it has holed in, or the sinker snagged in the rocks. Then a slow movement is felt and you can guess a large ling cod has taken hold of the fish.

As you raise it the ling cod bears down with its large pectoral fins, but does not move forward. It is a heavy deadweight pull to

92

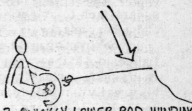

RAISE ROD -- KEEP LINE FROM RUNNING OUT.

2. QUICKLY LOWER ROD, WINDING IN LINE AT SAME TIME, TAKE UP SLACK. REPEAT 1-2-1-2 ETC.

bring the fish to the surface, alternately holding the line and raising the rod with all the force the rod will bear, then lowering the rod while reeling in the slack. Oddly, it makes no attempt to go down in the interval when the pressure is eased.

Eventually on the surface, it will lie there motionless with its jaws across the rockfish,

while you wonder what next to do. Unlike a large salmon, who is finished when brought to the boatside, the ling cod has not started to fight, apparently unaware of the danger he is in, despite being forced up from the dim depths and a pressure of 50 pounds per square inch to bright sunlight, no pressure and a boat nearby.

A rockfish brought up from that depth fights most of the way up, then floats helpless on the surface, unable to descend because of his greatly distended air sac. No so the ling cod. He lies there, not from gas in his stomach or loss of physical strength but apparently from mental dullness and obstinacy. Down below he is lord of all he surveys and no one is going to take that rockfish from him. The older and larger they get the more obstinate they become.

In the first two experiences of this nature the ling cod were not as large as in the third and let go on reaching the surface. The third was much larger, around 50 pounds, and lay motionless on the surface, holding on to his, or my, rockfish. I gaffed him under the lower jaw. He apparently felt nothing whatsoever for he made no movement nor showed any sign of discomfort. It was when I started to lift him that he went beserk, threw water all over me, bent the gaff and made off!

Most of my fishing was done from a small boat or a larger one with a cockpit too small to share with a large and lively ling cod.

After that episode, I always carried a towline in the tackle box. It was made up of a large hook attached to a strong line with a length of rubber to cushion a sudden jerk. A large fish could then be towed to a beach and safely landed. Think twice before you gaff a large ling cod or halibut from a small boat.

Anyone who has handled a rockfish and been pricked by one of the many sharp spines

on the dorsal fin will know how painful it can be. It seems to me that a fish that can swallow one alive has little feeling in its mouth, throat or stomach.

One large ling cod, who seized my rockfish, let go when I tried to hook him with the towline. He then made repeated splashing attacks on the fish lying on the surface, three feet from the boat, trying to get it by the head so he could swallow it. He must have been pricked, but showed no sign. After several tries he gave up and leisurely submerged.

On another occasion I had nearly all the fish we needed when a ling cod grabbed what was to have been the last fish. Pulling him to the surface I tapped him lightly on the head to make him let go but had to give a harder blow before he would leave.

Again in the summer of 1968 I was reeling in after a bite when a large ling cod took hold. On getting him to the surface all I could see was a small part of the rubber squid projecting from his jaws, so presumed he was hooked to my rod line. After a short attempt to tow him to shore he disgorged a four-and-three-quarter-pound ling cod, hooked to the squid -- likely one of his own offspring -- which I netted.

Four days later the same thing happened, possibly the same fish. This time there was no sign of the lure, the line coming straight from this tightly closed jaws. Again I thought

he must be hooked. Putting the rod in the rod rest, I had towed him a considerable distance toward shore, when the line slackened and I reeled in an unconscious five pound ling cod bearing the tooth marks of his elder.

I feel here I must speak up for the young people. I have always felt it unwise and even unkind to take them salmon fishing for their first fishing experience. I would not exchange those early adventures with sticklebacks and small roach for many of the trips for salmon taken since. They are happy memories of quiet ponds and small streams, moorhens, kingfishers and water rats;

butterflies, dragonflies, swallows and great expectations. These small adventures are appreciated only when young; to miss them then is to miss them forever.

Salmon fishing is for grownups. They can sit still for hours expecting something big to happen. Young people like smaller events happening more frequently.

The boat goes on and on, hour after hour, Dad says, "Can't you keep still, do you have to keep moving around." For the older ones a welcome rest, for the younger a bore. They get more excitement lying on a wharf trying to get the shiners they can see below.

They might be even happier if their Dad took part. He will find it takes knowledge and attention to catch shiners and hold the love and respect of children.

My wife Marjorie started her interest in fishing in this same way. On our first fishing trip together she brought along cushions and a book. I intended to get rockfish or ling cod and the only baits I knew of then were the natural ones, so tied the boat to the pilings of a wharf to catch shiners. Shiners are not easy to hook. One can watch them getting the bait off the hook but to land them takes experience.

After watching my futile attempts for awhile, Marjorie said, "Let me try," and that was it, she was hooked.

Salmon trolling and drifting for rockfish each have their pleasures and drawbacks.

Trolling for salmon is restful, the motor purring, I hope, while you sit back enjoying the sunshine and scenery, the gulls, ducks and divers, and if lucky have an interval of excitement landing a fish.

Drift fishing calls for constant attention every minute, keeping contact with the rough, rocky contours below. A little inattention and you may get snagged. With the slowly drifting boat there is no engine noise, just quietness and a feeling of expectation and mild excitement. Of the two kinds of entertainment, the latter is most appealing to the young. There is constant action they can take part in and with skill and experience there is a better than ten to one chance of getting fish. This, to the young, is the purpose of fishing.

On retirement at 69, fishing records were kept for 15 years, listing date, area, number, species and weights of all fish caught. According to the diaries the average number of reef fish caught per trip nearly doubled and the fruitless trips reduced from one in four to one in thirty, the average for the first eight years, and the last seven. I should mention that in the first eight years much time was spent salmon trolling and fishing with natural baits.

In the last seven years, making an average of 26 trips a year, from March to November, had only two blank days in one year, one blank in each of four years and no blank days in two. Rubber imitations of squid or octopus were used exclusively.

During 1969, the last full year of fishing, making 24 trips: no blanks; 17 ling cod and 57 rockfish were taken. Total weight was 452¾ pounds, an average of 18.8 pounds per trip, which when filleted would yield about six and a half pounds of fillets. A lingcod yields a full third of its weight in fillets without skin or bones; a rockfish slightly under one third.

Some trips only one fish was taken, but more often we stopped fishing when four or five or one large one were landed. We kept enough fillets for three meals for my wife and I and some for near neighbors who in turn gave us fruit and vegetables.

We did not freeze any fish, believing it better to leave them in the sea and get them fresh when needed.

Being retired it was possible to go out any time in the week when conditions were right and many times we took all we needed within an hour's actual fishing.

This greatly increased catch over former years was due to six factors:

1. Not spending time on salmon;
2. Not using fishing time to get natural bait;
3. Using vertically operated rubber imitations of squid and octopus, properly rigged;
4. Fishing in deeper water;

5. Finding unknown rocky outcrops in a large area of mud and fixing their positions by observing and recording landmarks; and
6. Discovering that rockfish in some areas feed on the rising tide and others maybe only a few hundred yards away, feed on the falling tide.

No doubt many experienced anglers have discovered this fact, but I have never seen it mentioned in the few books available dealing with rockfish.

It is well known that fish in a stream lie in the eddy behind boulders, darting out into the flowing water to capture passing food and returning to their resting place. Apparently dwellers among the rocks on the sea bottom also do this.

Where a rocky point runs out from the shore into deep water and the tide flows over it, most fish will be found feeding on the lee side of the ridge; this holds true for rocky

islands or any rocky prominence on the bottom. It is fortunate this is so, because where the fish are feeding, the boat is drifting from high ground to lower so the chances of getting snagged are much less than if one drifts from low to high ground. To make it clear, most fish living on one side of an undersea prominence feed on the rising tide and fish on the other side feed on a falling tide, in each case sheltered from the flowing water.

This is not to say no fish will be caught when drifting over a rising sea bottom. Some may be taken but not nearly so many.

My experience is that fish living around rocks do not feed when the water is stationary, high or low, or when it is moving at a speed which makes it difficult to keep contact with the bottom. A moderate tidal movement is best, rising or falling. Whether it is because the fish are too sedentary to face fast water, or the rubber squid tentacles do not behave in a lifelike manner in fast water, is a question. Heavier sinkers and weighted lures might work. The lure should drop head first, after the sinker strikes bottom.

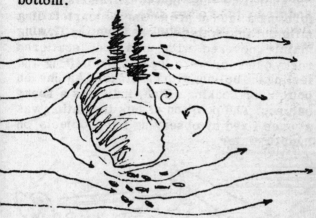

When fishing around a small island, the fish along the sides will be found feeding during a moderate current. When speed increases they stop, but may be found to bite in the lee of the island.

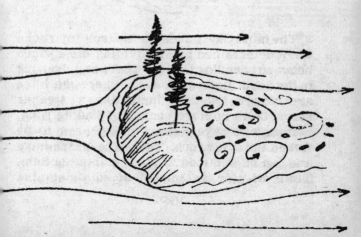

I have presumed that rockfish in other areas behave as they do in the area of Haro Strait where I fished.

There a wide rocky point pushing out from the shoreline runs downward under water, forming a mound projecting a quarter of a mile out into water 120 feet deep. This is mainly covered with mud, but scattered rocky outcrops were located by drifting and feeling the bottom with the sinker. An uneven bottom, or hooking a fish, indicates a rocky outcrop. The position of this indication was at once fixed by observing fixed objects on land or water.

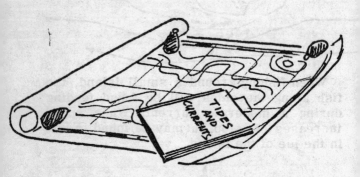

The most likely areas to search for rocks were determined by subdividing the spaces between soundings on the chart and drawing in the depth lines so found. Where the lines are closer together indicating a steeper slope, there is more chance of finding rock.

It pays to have a chart of the area to be fished and a tide book. These are inexpensive and can be obtained at most marine outlets. Time of tide is important to determine feeding times and varies greatly from station to station where tide recordings are made.

Most charts show depth lines at three, six, ten and twenty fathoms. To know, when out on the water, where you are in relation to these lines on the chart, it pays to cut the reel line at these four points, measuring from the sinker, and tying together again with blood (twist) knots.

As the line runs out, the knots can be counted with a finger. A further help is to color the knots, six, ten, and twenty, with different colors of enamel.

The most productive fishing is from a boat, drifting with the tide in water 60 to 120 feet or more deep. You can use handlines with heavier sinkers, but a short stiff rod about five feet in length, with a free spool, multiplying reel of the bay fishing type is much more satisfactory.

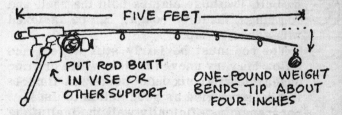

When the rod I use is fastened in a horizontal position, a weight of one pound hung from the top ring deflects the tip four inches from the horizontal; this is the stiffness recommended.

In the last nine years of boat fishing I have taken 2,540 lbs. of rockfish, ling cod and salmon on homemade lures and a rod made from seasoned spirea (Spiraea discolor) a common shrub around Victoria. This wood when seasoned for a year is much like cane, strong and springy. This rod was made from solid spirea wood, cut from a large stem, but a good rod can be made from a suitable shoot,

RUBBER HOSE BUTT
ON SPIRAEA
ROD.

five feet long and a full half inch diameter at the butt, cut in the fall, seasoned, and straightened if necessary with steam, with 18 inches of old rubber garden hose slipped over the butt. Two hose clamps hold the reel, and rod rings, made or bought, can be fastened with adhesive tape.

The rod must be fairly stiff to feel and follow the very uneven bottom while drifting on the tide with a six ounce sinker. A flexible rod does not give as good action to the lure nor transmit sufficiently well the feel of the bottom. When a sudden rise is encountered, it will not raise the weight quickly enough to avoid snagging. When a large rockfish bites, it must be lifted immediately and held or it may hole in; this a flexible rod cannot do.

Trolling and casting rods are usually operated from 45 degrees to vertical. When

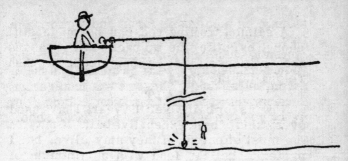

drift fishing the rod should be held horizontally when the sinker is on the ground, adjusting the reel to keep it so as the depth changes. Hooking and lifting a fish may raise the rod to around 45 degrees but never vertical.

Since the reel is positioned on trolling rods some distance from the butt, it is rather far from the body when horizontal. A shortened butt is more comfortable. An overall length of five ft. is recommended, especially in a dinghy.

The salmon fisherman who might like to get rockfish or ling cod when the salmon are not biting can use his trolling rod as it is by running the line through the lower rings and dropping it out through a ring one or two short of the tip. If used in this way frequently the ring from which the line drops should be replaced with a porcelain one to save wear on the line.

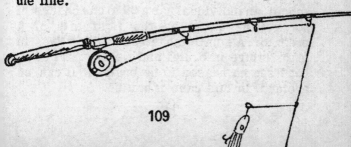

A salmon trolling rod can be made stiff enough by cutting the tip back until it passes the stiffness test recommended, then relocating the rings.

BAIT

Now, as for bait. Over the years I have used every kind of bait, except live bait. It may be the most effective, if they stay alive, but I prefer to get the food with a minimum of suffering. True, small fish get eaten by larger and they in turn by us, but to force a captive small fish, a hook through its back, alone into what it knows is an extremely dangerous area, to be killed or eventually die trying to escape, is unnecessary cruelty.

Most small fish, like birds in flocks, move in schools, for protection -- there are more eyes to spot enemies. If there are 100 fish in a school, an individual has a 99 to one chance of not getting eaten by the first bite of a predator. A small fish tethered alone lives in fear. Nature is brutal and we are part of it, but I see no reason to be brutal if it can be avoided. In this case it can be.

Most people like to see fish free in the water, also as food on the table. The unavoidable action between should be cut to a minimum. Always take a club along to dispatch the fish quickly. It is less protracted than being eaten alive, its most likely fate.

PUT ONE ARM OF HOOK IN NOTCH; PULL LINE TAUT

A serviceable club and hook extractor can be made from a seasoned spirea shoot, 15 inches long, of a size to fit tightly into a five inch length of half-inch galvanized iron water pipe. The pipe should be secured with a wedge in a saw cut at one end and the other end of the wood tapered, flattened and notched to engage the hook.

Frozen herring or any natural bait, to be effective, must be used fresh. They may not be on hand when needed; take time to get (which time could be better spent catching fish); and cannot be used twice. Worst of all, because dogfish hunt by smell, and bottom fish by sight, the likelihood of getting dogfish

SNIF!

SNIF!

instead of rockfish is much increased. They will follow a scent of blood, stale fish or worms, from a considerable distance. I doubt they would investigate the smell of rubber, although they will take hold if they see a rubber lure in action.

Dogfish are very good food, fried or boiled and made into fishcakes. Westerners are prejudiced. Our dog was not; quite the contrary.

Considering the abundance of bottom fish in our waters, it is astonishing that there is so little gear, specialized for their capture, available in our local stores. The rods

displayed are much too long and flexible for bottom fishing in deep water, where the larger fish are. They are useful when fishing from shore or boat in water less than 40 feet deep, where casting is the best method. Using the very numerous horizontally operated lures, much gear is lost because of the horizontal movement, and the necessity of getting close to the bottom.

Drift fishing, with vertically operated lures, is not so productive in depths under 30 feet. It is likely the boat being close above the

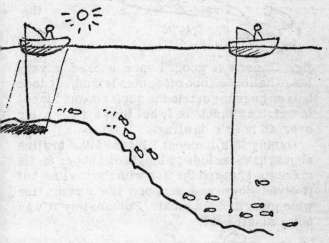

lure puts the fish off feeding. At greater depths the boat is not so visible nor so threatening. Some fish can be taken by casting well away from the boat into water the boat has not passed over.

I believe I am right in saying that almost all of the exceedingly numerous lures displayed in local stores are designed solely for trolling or casting horizontally so are not very efficient in a deep water vertical drop.

The two exceptions are Mike's Snagless Cod Jigger and the Norwegian plated lead cod

113

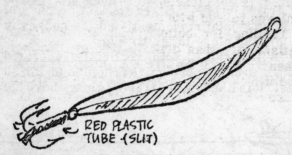

RED PLASTIC
TUBE (SLIT)

jig. These are good. I once hooked a very
large halibut on one off James Island. It took
half an hour to get it to the surface, and looked
to weigh as much as I, but broke away after
over an hour's battling.

During this incident I learned the towline
should have included a length of rubber in its
makeup. I hooked the fish with the towline but
it dived down and snapped the strong line
which was tied to a cleat. Fortunately it was
not a small boat.

SPUNG!

The drawback to this cod jig is that the
hooks unavoidably strike bottom, catch
weeds, snag on rocks, and must be raised

frequently to check for weeds. This, in deep water, takes time better employed catching fish. It is not pleasing to wonder how many fish you passed with a weedy lure.

Trolling for bottom fish is far less satisfactory than drift fishing or casting. When trolling, if the lure is too deep, it snags. And if less deep, misses most of the fish since only the high spots are fished.

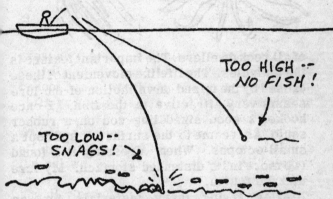

As mentioned earlier, when fishing in water less than 40 feet deep, casting is a fairly good way to get bottom fish. The lures available, (Buzz Bombs, plugs, spoons, etc.), are effective, but when fishing in water over 40 feet deep, drifting on the tide with the line as vertical as the current will allow is more productive. Use lures, rigging and sinkers designed for vertical action, in deep water on a rough bottom, and you will get larger fish and more of them, with less loss of tackle, than casting in the shallower water.

BEST LURE

The lures I found best of all were close imitations of squid or octopus, a favorite food

of all rock dwellers. The important feature is the tentacles. The lifelike movement of these caused by the up and down motion of the lure seems very attractive to the fish. I once hooked a good sized ling cod on a rubber squid. As it came to the surface it spat out a small octopus. When dressing it I found two more in its distended stomach. My lure was the fourth.

After trying many materials for an imitation squid or octopus, including lifelike imitations of Pacific squid made with latex rubber, the best on all points for the amateur craftsman was the finger of a rubber glove,

large size for deep water and smaller for where smaller fish are.

The color is not important. Squid and octopus can change color quickly from dull white to dark red. I have had equal success with near-white, yellow, pink and red. This lure really simulates a small octopus.

A pair of gloves will give material for ten lures (about ten cents each). To restore the roundness of the fingers which have been flattened by storage, fill the glove with very hot water, then cold.

The only tools essential to make the lures are:

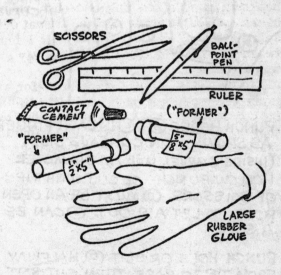

HOW TO MAKE
GIRLING'S OCTOPUS LURE

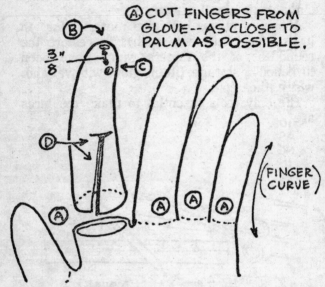

(A) CUT FINGERS FROM GLOVE -- AS CLOSE TO PALM AS POSSIBLE.

3/8"

(FINGER CURVE)

PUNCH HOLES (B) & (C) IN EACH FINGER AS SHOWN -- ON CONCAVE SIDE. (INSIDE CURVE). USE 1/8" DIAMETER HOLLOW PUNCH -- OR CUT WITH TIP OF SCISSORS. (B) MUST BE AN OPEN HOLE TO LET AIR OUT. (C) CAN BE A SLIT.

PUNCH HOLE OR SLIT (D) HALFWAY FROM TIP TO BASE. THEN CUT SLIT FROM BASE TO HOLE

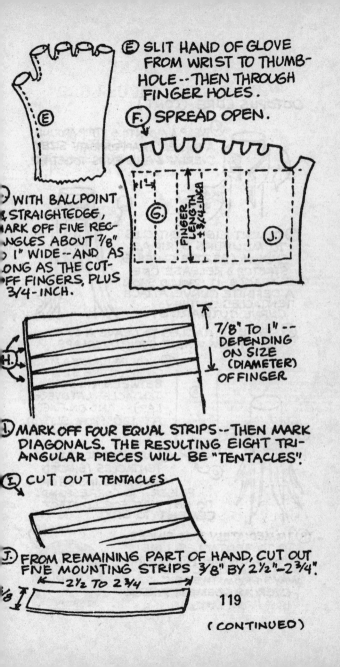

E. SLIT HAND OF GLOVE FROM WRIST TO THUMB-HOLE -- THEN THROUGH FINGER HOLES.

F. SPREAD OPEN.

G. WITH BALLPOINT & STRAIGHTEDGE, MARK OFF FIVE RECTANGLES ABOUT 7/8" TO 1" WIDE -- AND AS LONG AS THE CUT-OFF FINGERS, PLUS 3/4-INCH.

FINGER LENGTH + 3/4-INCH

7/8" TO 1" -- DEPENDING ON SIZE (DIAMETER) OF FINGER

H. MARK OFF FOUR EQUAL STRIPS -- THEN MARK DIAGONALS. THE RESULTING EIGHT TRI-ANGULAR PIECES WILL BE "TENTACLES"!

I. CUT OUT TENTACLES

J. FROM REMAINING PART OF HAND, CUT OUT FIVE MOUNTING STRIPS 3/8" BY 2½"-2¾".

3/8

2½ TO 2¾

119

(CONTINUED)

OCTOPUS LURE (CONT.)

K. WRAP A MOUNTING STRIP AROUND A "FORMER" OF APPROPRIATE SIZE. OVERLAP & GLUE ENDS TOGETHER.

CONTACT CEMENT

L. CEMENT EIGHT TENTACLES TO MOUNTING STRIP AS SHOWN. (BEFORE GLUEING, STRETCH & RELEASE ONE TENTACLE. IT SHOULD SHOW A DEFINITE CURVE. ATTACH TENTACLES SO THEY CURVE OUTWARDS.

M. SPACE TENTACLES TO LEAVE A GAP 180° FROM WHERE STRIP OVERLAPS.

N. WITH PEN, MAKE A MARK ON MOUNTING STRIP BETWEEN 4th & 5th TENTACLES (AT OVERLAP) -- AND ON FINGER AT 180° FROM SLIT ⓓ.

O. APPLY CEMENT TO TENTACLES (SHADED AREAS) AND INSIDE OF FINGER -- TO CORRESPOND. DO NOT WAIT FOR CONTACT CEMENT TO DRY!

P. IMMEDIATELY JOIN FINGER TO TENTACLES. LINE UP MARKS ON MOUNTING STRIP AND FINGER. WORK BOTH WAYS FROM THERE. OVERLAP & CEMENT FINGER 180° FROM MARKS.

FINGER

MOUNTING STRIP

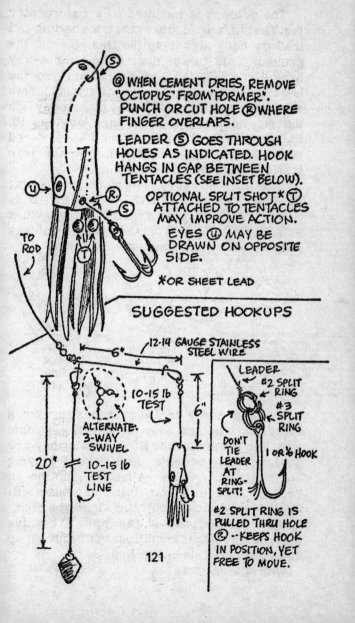

@ WHEN CEMENT DRIES, REMOVE "OCTOPUS" FROM "FORMER". PUNCH OR CUT HOLE ®WHERE FINGER OVERLAPS.

LEADER ⑤ GOES THROUGH HOLES AS INDICATED. HOOK HANGS IN GAP BETWEEN TENTACLES (SEE INSET BELOW).

OPTIONAL SPLIT SHOT *⑪ ATTACHED TO TENTACLES MAY IMPROVE ACTION.

EYES ⓤ MAY BE DRAWN ON OPPOSITE SIDE.

*OR SHEET LEAD

TO ROD

SUGGESTED HOOKUPS

12-14 GAUGE STAINLESS STEEL WIRE

6"

10-15 lb TEST

6"

ALTERNATE: 3-WAY SWIVEL

20"

10-15 lb TEST LINE

LEADER

#2 SPLIT RING

#3 SPLIT RING

DON'T TIE LEADER AT RING-SPLIT!

1 OR ⅙ HOOK

#2 SPLIT RING IS PULLED THRU HOLE ® --KEEPS HOOK IN POSITION, YET FREE TO MOVE.

121

The octopus is mounted on a paternoster rig. That is, a lead sinker to strike bottom and the lure hung higher up the line clear of the ground. This can be done from a three-way swivel about 20″ above the sinker, so the hooks are about a foot above the ground. This works fairly well, and I have caught many fish that way but sometimes the lure tangles with the main line. This rig should be lowered while the boat is still moving so the lure trails away from the main line.

This lure is very effective in hooking because when the fish bites, the body collapses and ensures a good hooking. When extracting the hook from the fish, the octopus can be slid up the line out of the way.

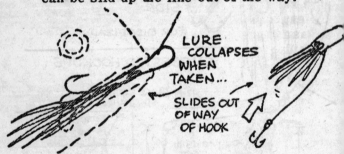

LURE COLLAPSES WHEN TAKEN...

SLIDES OUT OF WAY OF HOOK

No doubt some trolling or casting lures rigged on a paternoster boom will get some fish, but, except for the Buzz Bomb, they are designed to deceive fish when moving horizontally. With vertical motion a resemblance to some living creature will happen only occasionally in sight of a fish. The rubber octopus looks and acts like a live octopus whether it is stationary or moving up and down, so gets more fish.

With this rig I use a 30-lb. test nylon reel line, so if the sinker snags only the sinker is lost and the same with the lure.

The sinker is best spherical or egg shaped, forms that give most weight with least surface area. It moves easily through the water when keeping up with the drifting boat.

The tidal flow is faster at the surface than on the bottom so there is always some slant to the line. This should be kept to a minimum by avoiding fast water.

In 60 feet or less I use a four-ounce sinker, in 60 feet to 120 feet a six-ounce. These weights were satisfactory in my area where the deepest reef was 120 feet down and tidal flow rarely too strong.

Heavier sinkers might be needed in other areas and more split shot clamped on to the hook link.

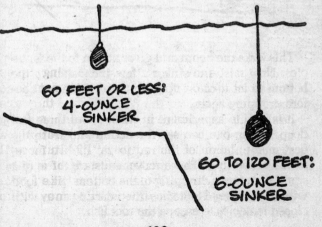

60 FEET OR LESS:
4-OUNCE
SINKER

60 TO 120 FEET:
6-OUNCE
SINKER

When the sinker reaches bottom, lower the line a few more inches to allow the boom to drop and give time for the octopus to reach its tentacles-down position. Then give a few rod tip movements — quick up and slow down — without lifting the sinker from the bottom.

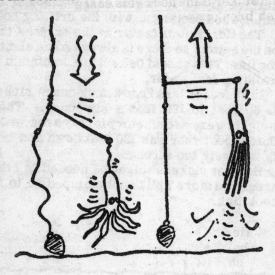

This jerks the boom and gives action to the tentacles. Now raise the sinker a few inches above the bottom to let it catch up with the drifting boat before dropping again.

It is well to experiment in water about three feet deep, where one can see the action and learn the best manipulation of the rod to get lifelike movements of the lure. These movements are those of a squid or octopus dropping to the bottom to get food with its outspread tentacles, then darting away with closed tentacles to escape the rockfish.

Although dogfish are less bother with artificial lures, they are troublesome enough to make it worthwhile to use some wire in the hook link. The wire should connect to the boom with a short piece of nylon to save boom and sinker if the hook gets snagged or a large fish breaks away.

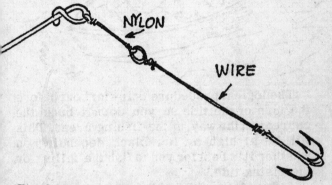

NYLON

WIRE

Be alert to every up and down contour of the rocks below, reeling in or letting out as the depth changes, keeping the rod as near horizontal as possible so if a fish bites it can be lifted immediately and held from holing in.

If snagged while drifting, row back well beyond where the sinker caught and there is a good chance it can be pulled free.

Because the fish bite either on a rising or falling tide, depending on the slope of the reef, it pays to choose the tidal movement which will drift you toward home while handling a large fish. Otherwise you have to row against the tide to get back to the reef, also against the tide all the way home. If the drift takes you toward home while landing the last fish there is that much less rowing to get there.

The logical procedure is to start out before the turn of the tide so you do not buck the current on the way to the fishing area. This will be at high or low slack depending on whether it is best for you to fish the falling or the rising tide.

Although the tide tables give the time of high and low water at spaced locations, it does not follow that the current turns at those times, or that there is a steadily increasing or decreasing current in between those times.

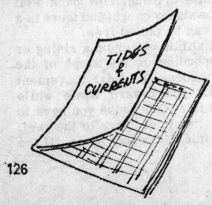

Often when the rise or fall is only a few feet, the water may be stationary for a while, before, at, or after the forecast times. It may speed up or slow down during the rise or fall and the fish may come on and go off feeding as the current moves, slows and moves again.

Awareness of these facts added to some experience will help you get fish more often. Whenever you get a bite note tidal conditions as well as location.

A boat designed for easy rowing is good for reef fishing. It is manoeuverable and excellent exercise, equal to a rowing machine but more pleasant and profitable. When fishing from a rowboat the oars should be tied to the gunwale. If an oar gets knocked overboard when one is getting a fish up from the deeps, it could be difficult to regain it. One oar is not every effective even in a light wind and tide.

It pays to make a fishbox the right size and shape to suit the boat's bottom, and that will push under the stern seat. This keeps the floor clear and less slippery. A large rockfish flopping around your ankles with spines erect diverts attention from the work in hand.

It is regrettable that practically all small boats these days are designed for outboard motors so do not move freely with oars and drift badly in wind. Maybe when the air is sufficiently polluted we will have good rowboats again.

Getting back to fish behavior; in addition to the influence of tidal movements on the fish's feeding times, weather conditions also have some effect. Izaac Walton observes in 'The

Compleat Angler' that trout do not bite so well during an easterly wind. I have found this to be true of rockfish.

But one never knows for sure. The year after selling my dinghy, a new neighbor, interested in fishing, asked if I would come along in her boat to get some experience in drift fishing.

By the time we had the boat launched, an east wind had started. By the time the reef was reached, it was really too strong for fishing. We got on the marks but the boat,

with wind and tide, drifted too fast for a controlled drop of over 100 feet, the line taking too long a slant.

Returning to the spot I decided to take a chance, letting the reel run completely free the whole distance, despite the danger of a bad overrun.

The sinker hit bottom and the overrun was not too bad. I reeled in the slack and there was a fish on. After netting it, a rockfish around five lbs., we returned to marks and tried again, with exactly the same result, a similar fish. By this time the sea was getting rough, so came in.

Sometimes when sufficient fish were caught and still time to spare, I searched for rocky outcrops using a rubber squid lure with no hooks.

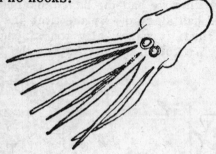

It was remarkable and amusing how the fish would grab the lure, make repeated runs, pulling the line quite strongly, then letting go. It would then be retaken immediately either by that fish or another.

One might object that fish would reject an artificial lure before the angler could strike the hook in, but apparently the rubber lure feels so like a squid or octopus that the fish retains it in its mouth.

Repeatedly when dropping the lure and sinker 100 ft. or more with some overrun, when the line was recovered a fish was already on, showing it did not at once reject the rubber lure as being something strange. Their reaction to a lead lure would likely be different.

It is possible to get a vertical drop when casting by using a specially designed sliding float.

Experiments were conducted to design a sliding float that, after casting a distance from the boat or shore, would drop and lift the lure vertically while moving slowly back. When reeled in fast the lure would rise to the surface and come home.

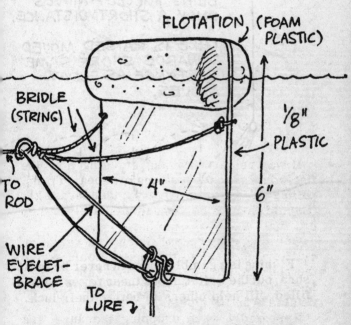

FLOTATION, (FOAM PLASTIC)

BRIDLE (STRING)

⅛" PLASTIC

TO ROD

4"

6"

WIRE EYELET-BRACE

TO LURE

SIDNEY GIRLING'S SLIDING FLOAT

CAST OFF SHORE, FLOAT'S LARGE, FLAT FACE RESISTS BEING PULLED THROUGH WATER. LINE IS FREE TO MOVE THROUGH EYELETS SO LURE CAN SINK TO DESIRED DEPTH, AND BE JIGGED, ETC.

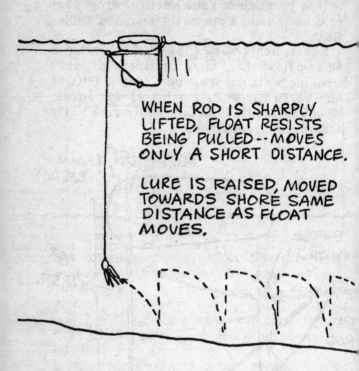

WHEN ROD IS SHARPLY
LIFTED, FLOAT RESISTS
BEING PULLED -- MOVES
ONLY A SHORT DISTANCE.

LURE IS RAISED, MOVED
TOWARDS SHORE SAME
DISTANCE AS FLOAT
MOVES.

Fishing is a gamble, one can never be quite sure, but the writer hopes these pages he has filled will help others to better their luck.

CHAPTER IX

PERCH

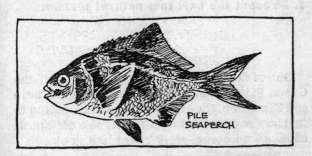

PILE
SEAPERCH

These colorful, mid-water swimmers are always a source of great excitement when a school is spotted cruising near a dock or mooage. The children, particularly, really love to catch these wily rascals.

The smaller Shiner Perch are usually easy to catch, but the larger Striped Perch and Pile Perch seem to ignore most baits dropped in front of their noses. This is especially true in bays and wharf areas where large numbers of pleasure boats

HOHUM...

congregate. The Perch are just too "wise".

There are several techniques which seem to produce results. In order to catch Perch, you should remember two things:

1. Find his natural food and prepare it so it is easy to eat.

2. Present the bait in a natural manner.

PERCH BAITS

One of the best baits is our old friend, the Green Pile Worm that is so effective for Sole and Flounder. (See Sole & Flounder section to find how to get pile worms.) Break off small chunks and completely cover the hook.

Tiny mussels, only ¼-inch to ½-inch across, are excellent Perch bait around docks and pilings where they are a large part of their natural food. Thread the mussel (whole in the shell) on the hook, breaking up the shell as little as possible.

Larger mussels can also be used, but must be broken into pieces and are not as effective. Be sure to leave the bits of shell clinging to the meat.

Shore crabs, the small crabs found by the thousands under rocks along the shore in the inter-tidal zone, are also good bait. Use small specimens and take off one or both

claws. (Perch prefer a meal that doesn't fight back too hard!) Hook the crab through the side of the shell so he can wiggle actively.

Ghost shrimp (see **Sole & Flounder** section) can be deadly for Perch. Use small ones whole and break large ones in half.

Clams, herring and other baits are sometimes used, but they are often ineffective.

PRESENTING THE BAIT

Perch are very "fussy" eaters, so the bait must be presented carefully and naturally:

1. **Use light line and small hooks** - A number 4 or 5 hook is about right. You can use line as light as 4- or 5-pound test, but I find 10-pound test to be light enough most places. You might use 10-pound line with 6-pound leader, tied with a tiny, tiny, swivel about 4 to 6 feet from the hook.

2. **Do Not use a sinker** - Letting the bait fall naturally through the water seems to be one

135

of the most important factors in catching Perch. A bait being dragged down by even a small split shot weight is enough to "scare off" most Perch. Let the bait fall freely to the bottom or through the fish school, then

retrieve and repeat the free fall process. No cast is necessary when dock fishing. Just drop the line in the water and keep it slack for free falling.

If you can't make the line sink without a weight (due to current), try tossing it upcurrent so it will drift down toward you, sinking as it comes. As a last resort, put a tiny weight right next to the swivel about 4 feet from the bait.

3. Keep yourself inconspicuous - Perch can see you as well or better than you can see

them. Don't make sudden moves or wave your arms to point out the school to your friends. Talking or even shouting won't disturb the fish since sound waves don't carry well into water. Any stamping, banging, or vibration on the dock (or boat) however, will be carried instantly into the water and might scare the fish.

4. Look for the fish - If you lie down on the dock with your face near the water, and in the shade, you will usually be able to see the school of Perch. Anticipate their direction and drop your bait to flutter down a few feet in front of them. If your bait is right, several Perch should rush up to inspect it and one will suck it into his mouth!

5. Try different times of day - Like all fish, Perch feed more actively at certain times. Early morning and evening are often good times. In busy marinas, try the times when not many boats are moving and things are peaceful and quiet.

CHAPTER X

SURF PERCH

These sporty fighters are quite similar to their quiet water cousins, but they live in a much more active environment. They are found in the active surf off rocky or sandy shorelines along the open coast. They are not shy, fussy eaters like their relatives, but will grab aggressively at baits presented to them.

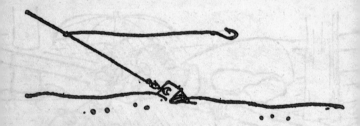

Casting or spinning outfits are best for this type of fishing. Use a rig with a sinker at the extreme end.

Clams, mussels, and pile worms are good bait. Fishermen are also reporting excellent catches using Dungeness crab legs for bait!

CHAPTER XI

GREENLING
("KELP COD" "KELP TROUT")

These sporty fish are most often found around kelp beds and rocky shorelines. They have a small mouth and smaller hooks (No. 2 to 4) are often effective with bait. They will also strike small artificial lures. A wet fly cast with a spinning outfit and retrieved slowly near the bottom can produce good results. They are not an important fish to either the sport or commercial fisherman.

ROCK GREENLING

CHAPTER XII

JIGGING WITH ARTIFICIAL LURES

Jigging is increasingly popular for salmon fish-ing, with newer and more sophisticated lures moving in to compete with the traditional Buzz-Bombs, Stingsildas, Pirkens and many others. These jigs have always been effective for bottomfish as well and, using techniques discovered in experiments with our underwater camera, can be even more so.

Jigging with artificial lures imitates the action of severely wounded or stunned baitfish which just flutter down toward the bottom. A shorter, somewhat stiffer rod is best, and there are many different jigging strokes used.

I had the opportunity to talk and fish with the late

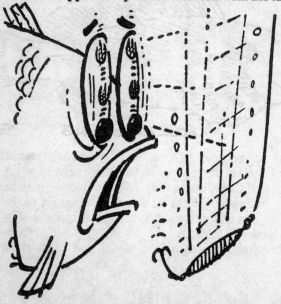

Rex Field, pioneer developer of the Buzz-Bomb. He told me that most people jerk his lures far too hard. "Fish can't catch a jigg that's moving too fast,"

claimed Rex. Our underwater camera proved him correct.

We found that salmon and bottomfish would make one or two passes at the lure, then give up quickly if they didn't catch it. To our surprise, even short pulls were difficult to catch, and we set out to design jigs which would flutter down more slowly and be easier to catch.

We tried lures of lighter metal and lures with

plastic "wings," but they were too hard to control and get an effective action. Then we added a forked spinner, similar to the one used on our trolling lure. It worked well. The spinner acted like a parachute and slowed the lure just enough that the fish caught

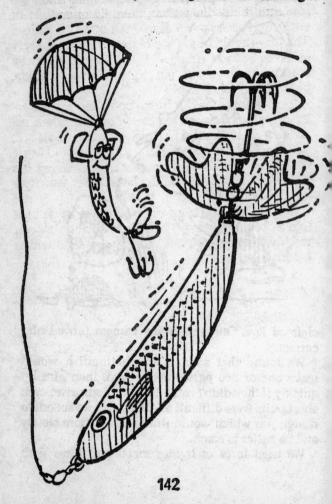

it much more easily. As a bonus, the flash of the spinner and the sonic vibration focussed the strike at the tail of the lure where our sticky sharp hooks were waiting.

Jigging for bottomfish is quite simple. Drop the lure until it hits the bottom, then jig up and down with short strokes—no more than 12 to 18 inches. The lure should bump the bottom on almost every stroke to be most effective. When jigging on rocky bottoms, the lures will get scarred up very quickly, but they still catch fish.

As mentioned earlier in the book, the productivity of jigging lures more than doubled when we added a small chunk of bait to the hooks. This bait was especially true with Sole, Flounder, and other flatfish. A couple of short jigs, then leaving the baited lure motionless on the bottom was usually a deadly technique.

Jigging lures are often more effective when bent into a "banana" shape. This bend allows a slower, wobbly flutter which our camera showed stimulated strike activity.

HOW TO CLEAN & FILLET BOTTOMFISH
(ROCK FISH, SNAPPER, LINGCOD, ETC.)

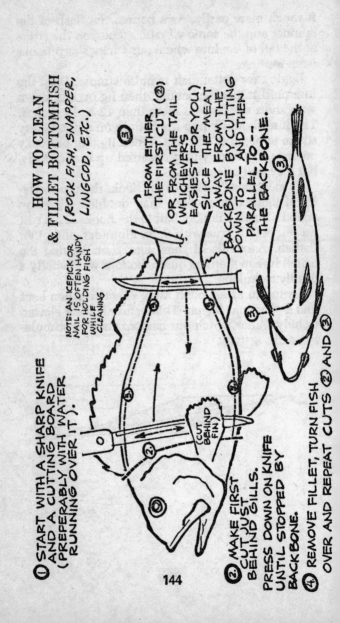

① START WITH A SHARP KNIFE AND A CUTTING BOARD (PREFERABLY WITH WATER RUNNING OVER IT).

② MAKE FIRST CUT JUST BEHIND GILLS. PRESS DOWN ON KNIFE UNTIL STOPPED BY BACKBONE.

(CUT BEHIND FIN)

NOTE: AN ICEPICK OR NAIL IS OFTEN HANDY FOR HOLDING FISH WHILE CLEANING

FROM EITHER THE FIRST CUT ② OR FROM THE TAIL (WHICHEVER'S EASIEST FOR YOU) SLICE THE MEAT AWAY FROM THE BACKBONE BY CUTTING DOWN TO -- AND THEN PARALLEL TO -- THE BACKBONE.

④ REMOVE FILLET, TURN FISH OVER AND REPEAT CUTS ② AND ③

144

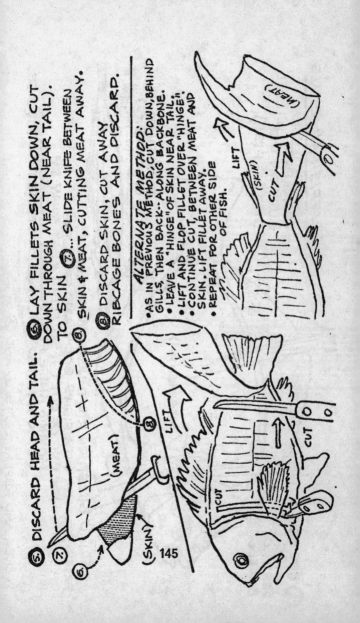

⑤ DISCARD HEAD AND TAIL.

⑥ LAY FILLETS SKIN DOWN, CUT DOWN THROUGH MEAT (NEAR TAIL). TO SKIN

⑦ ... SLIDE KNIFE BETWEEN SKIN & MEAT, CUTTING MEAT AWAY.

⑧ DISCARD SKIN, CUT AWAY RIBCAGE BONES AND DISCARD.

(MEAT)

(SKIN)

LIFT

CUT

ALTERNATE METHOD:

- AS IN PREVIOUS METHOD, CUT DOWN, BEHIND GILLS, THEN BACK-- ALONG BACKBONE.
- LEAVE A "HINGE" OF SKIN NEAR TAIL.
- LIFT AND FLOP FILLET OVER "HINGE".
- CONTINUE CUT, BETWEEN MEAT AND SKIN. LIFT FILLET AWAY.
- REPEAT FOR OTHER SIDE OF FISH.

(MEAT)

(SKIN)

LIFT

CUT

145

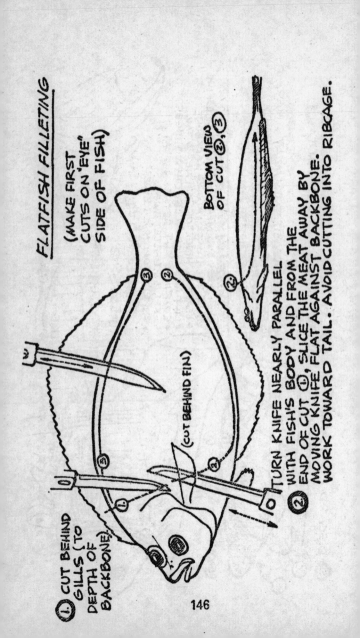

FLATFISH FILLETING

(MAKE FIRST CUTS ON "EYE" SIDE OF FISH)

BOTTOM VIEW OF CUT ②, ③

(CUT BEHIND FIN)

① CUT BEHIND GILLS (TO DEPTH OF BACKBONE).

② TURN KNIFE NEARLY PARALLEL WITH FISH'S BODY AND FROM THE END OF CUT ①, SLICE THE MEAT AWAY BY MOVING KNIFE FLAT AGAINST BACKBONE. WORK TOWARD TAIL. AVOID CUTTING INTO RIBCAGE.

146

③ REPEAT PREVIOUS CUT, BUT FROM TOP OF FISH'S BACK, STARTING AT BEGINNING OF CUT ①.

④ PEEL MEAT & SKIN AWAY FROM FISH -- STILL ATTACHED NEAR THE TAIL -- AND LAY IT OUT FLAT.

⑤ CUT MEAT AWAY FROM THE SKIN. PEEL MEAT AWAY AS YOU MAKE CUT -- THEN CLEAN ANY FIN, INTESTINE, RIB BONES FROM THE MEAT.

⑥ TURN FISH OVER, REPEAT ① THRU ⑤. (IF YOU WISH, THE "BOTTOM" SKIN CAN BE LEFT ON THE MEAT, AS IT'S USUALLY QUITE TENDER.

⑦ DISCARD HEAD & BONES; COOK OR FREEZE MEAT TO SUIT.

* LARGER FISH -- SUCH AS HALIBUT -- ARE USUALLY GUTTED AND CUT CROSSWAYS INTO STEAKS OR CHUNKS.

147

Fishing Diary

DATE	TIME	LURE AND COLOR	DEPTH	WEATHER - TIDE

SPECIES - WEIGHT - WHERE

Fishing Diary

DATE	TIME	LURE AND COLOR	DEPTH	WEATHER - TIDE

SPECIES - WEIGHT - WHERE

Look for these books of outdoor exploration and discovery to help you get the most from B.C.'s great outdoors!

Available at your bookstore or sporting goods store — or you can order them from Heritage House Publishing Company on the convenient order form at the end of this book.

HOW TO CATCH BOTTOMFISH
by Charles White
While salmon are the "glamour" fish, bottomfish are tasty and easy to catch. This book shows how to catch cod, sole, perch, snapper, rockfish, and other bottomfish. Best tackle and rigs, baits, when and where to fish. Detailed step-by-step filleting diagrams.

Revised 5th printing   160 pages $5.95

HOW TO CATCH CRABS
by Captain Crabwelle
This book, revised to show the latest crabbing techniques, describes how to catch crabs with traps, scoops, and rings; where and when to set traps; the best baits to use. It includes a detailed description of an easier, improved method of cleaning, cooking and shelling the meat. It's a great book, crammed with everything you need to know about catching crabs.

Updated 11th printing   110 pages $4.95

HOW TO CATCH SHELLFISH
by Charles White
How, when and where to find and catch many forms of tasty shellfish: oysters, clams, shrimp, mussels, limpets. Easiest way to shuck oysters. Best equipment for clamming and shrimping. When not to eat certain shellfish. What to eat and what to discard. A delightful book of useful information. Well illustrated.

Updated 4th printing   144 pages $3.95

HOW TO CATCH STEELHEAD

This book by popular outdoors writer Alec Merriman contains helpful information for novice or expert. Information includes how to "read" the water, proper bait, techniques for fishing clear or murky water, and fly fish for steelhead. Many diagrams and illustrations.

5th printing   112 pages $3.95

HOW TO FISH WITH DODGERS AND FLASHERS

Joined by guest authors Lee Straight, Jack Gaunt and Bruce Colegrave, Jim Gilbert helps you catch more salmon. Find out when to use a dodger or a flasher, all about bait and lure hookups, best lure action, trolling speeds, leader lengths and more.

2nd printing   128 pages $3.95

CHARLIE WHITE'S
101 SALMON FISHING SECRETS
by Charles White

Charlie shares more than a hundred of his special fishing secrets to help improve technique and increase your catch. No fisherman should pass this one up. Illustrated throughout with Nelson Dewey's distinctive cartoons and helpful diagrams.

Updated 3rd printing   144 pages $9.95

DRIFT FISHING

Seven expert Pacific Coast fishermen help you become more productive using Perkin, Buzz-Bomb, Stingsilda, Deadly Dick, and herring. Whether you fish salmon, bottomfish or trout this book of illustrated techniques for mooching, casting and jigging can increase your catch.

Revised 4th edition   160 pages   **$10.95**

HOW TO COOK YOUR CATCH
by Jean Challenger

Tells how to cook on board a boat, at a cabin or campsite. Shortcuts in preparing seafood for cooking, cleaning and filleting. Recipes and methods for preparing delicious meals using simple camp utensils. Special section on exotic seafoods. Illustrated.

8th printing   192 pages   **$4.95**

BUCKTAILS AND HOOCHIES

Trolling bucktail flies is one of the most exciting methods of catching salmon, as well as being very productive. Hoochies have always been the favorite of commercial fishermen and expert Jack Gaunt tells sportsmen how to catch salmon with them.

Updated 5th printing   112 pages   **$4.95**

HOW TO CATCH TROUT

Lee Straight is one of Western Canada's top outdoorsmen. Here he shares many secrets from his own experience and from experts with whom he has fished. Chapters include trolling, casting, ice fishing, best baits and lures, river and lake fishing methods — and much more.

8th printing   144 pages $5.95

AN EXPLORER'S GUIDE TO THE MARINE PARKS OF B.C.
by Peter Chettleburgh

The definitive guide to B.C.'s marine parks. Includes anchorages and onshore facilities, trails, picnic areas and campsites. Profusely illustrated with color and black and white photos, maps and charts, this is essential reading for all yachtsmen and small boat campers.

200 pages $12.95

LIVING OFF THE SEA
by Charles White

Detailed techniques for catching crabs, prawn, shrimp, sole, cod and other bottomfish; oysters, clams and more. How to clean, fillet, shuck — in fact everything you need to know to enjoy the freshest seafood in the world. Black and white photos and lots of helpful diagrams.

Updated 2nd printing   128 pages $7.95

FLY FISH THE TROUT LAKES
with Jack Shaw

Professional outdoor writers describe the author as a man "who can come away regularly with a string when everyone else has been skunked." In this book, he shares over 40 years of studying, raising and photographing all forms of lake insects and the behaviour of fish to them. Written in an easy-to-follow style.

2nd printing   96 pages $7.95

SALMON FISHING BRITISH COLUMBIA:
Volume One — Vancouver Island

Vancouver Island is one of the world's best year-round salmon fishing areas. This comprehensive guide describes popular fishing holes with a map of each and data on gear, best time of year, most productive fishing methods and much more.

128 pages $9.95

SALMON FISHING BRITISH COLUMBIA:
Volume Two — Mainland Coast

Detailed descriptions of nearly 100 fishing holes from Boundary Bay northward to Jervis Inlet, including Active and Porlier Passes, Burrard Inlet, Howe Sound, Gibsons, Lasquiti, Pender Harbour, Egmont and other waters. Information includes where to fish, gear, best lures, location maps and much more.

144 pages $11.95

LOWER MAINLAND BACKROADS

This informative series is a comprehensive mile-by-mile guide to highways and byways from Vancouver to the Cariboo-Thompson Country and includes the Garibaldi Region, Bridge River to Kamloops, the Thompson River and Cariboo Plateau.

LOWER MAINLAND BACKROADS:
Volume 1
— Bridge River Country, Garibaldi to Lillooet
by Richard Thomas Wright

Revised edition of a best seller. This detailed guide to highways and byways includes route mileage, fishing holes, wildlife, history, maps and many photos.

168 pages $9.95

LOWER MAINLAND BACKROADS:
Volume 3
— The Junction Country, Boston Bar to Clinton
by Richard Thomas Wright

A complete update of this best selling guide to the Interior Plateau country with its canoeing, fishing, gold panning, hunting, rockhounding and other outdoor activities. Detailed maps and many photos.

164 pages $9.95

BACKROADS EXPLORER:
Thompson-Cariboo
by Murphy Shewchuk

This comprehensive guide to the backroads of the Thompson-South Cariboo region is packed with information: points of scenic and historical interest; recreational facilities; best fishing areas; campsites and accommodation. Many photos and easy-to-follow maps.

176 pages $4.95

IN CLOSING — IMPORTANT REMINDER

As noted on page 4, before fishing B.C. tidal waters carefully check the current B.C. Tidal Waters Sport Fishing Guide, published annually by the Federal Department of Fisheries and Oceans. It is available free at sporting goods stores, marinas and similar outlets. The Guide contains all current regulations governing sport fishing not only for salmon but also for halibut, rockfish, crabs, oysters and other species. Check carefully the sections on spot closures which were introduced as a conservation measure to protect not only salmon but also crabs, lingcod and many other species.

BOOK ORDER FORM

Please send me the following books:

COPIES	TITLE	EACH	TOTAL
......	BUCKTAILS AND HOOCHIES	$ 4.95	......
......	CHARLE WHITE'S 101 FISHING SECRETS	$ 9.95	......
......	DRIFT FISHING	$10.95	......
......	EXPLORER'S GUIDE TO MARINE PARKS	$12.95	......
......	FLY FISH THE TROUT LAKES	$ 7.95	......
......	HOW TO CATCH BOTTOMFISH	$ 5.95	......
......	HOW TO CATCH CRABS	$ 4.95	......
......	HOW TO CATCH SALMON - Advanced	$11.95	......
......	HOW TO CATCH SALMON - Basic	$ 5.95	......
......	HOW TO CATCH SHELLFISH	$ 3.95	......
......	HOW TO CATCH STEELHEAD	$ 3.95	......